The Vital Heart of
CHRISTIANITY

formerly published as *Resurrection Realities*

MERRILL C. TENNEY, PH.D.

Dean of the Graduate School
Wheaton College, Illinois

Foreword by V. RAYMOND EDMAN, PH.D., LL.D.

ZONDERVAN PUBLISHING HOUSE
GRAND RAPIDS   MICHIGAN

Printed in the United States of America

TO MY STUDENTS

PAST AND PRESENT

WHO ARE FAITHFULLY PREACHING

THE GLORIOUS GOSPEL

OF A RISEN CHRIST

Foreword

MUCH of human thought concerns itself with matters which are secondary, and therefore are not intrinsically essential. Here is a studied and scholarly statement of the greatest question that faces the human mind. By training and reflection, the author is highly qualified to present a statement of the case that should be carefully considered by every reader.

Many have not faced the facts and implications of the resurrection of the Lord Jesus Christ, and they are urged thoughtfully to weigh the evidence herein presented. Others have come to know Christ for themselves and need this confirmation of the basic doctrine of the resurrection and clarification of their conclusions in that regard. In the classroom and on the campus, hundreds of young people have thought through this matter with the author, and have been established unshakably in the position, "Now is Christ Risen."

V. RAYMOND EDMAN

President of Wheaton College
Wheaton, Illinois

Introduction

THE title of this book represents the author's conviction that the essential truths of Christianity stem from the one stupendous event of the Resurrection of Jesus Christ. For this manifestation of divine power all the revelation of God in the Old Testament is preparatory; from this event originate the doctrines and dynamic of the Gospel. Christianity is not one more religion, invented to satisfy the spiritual vacuum in man's nature and born of cultural accident, but it was founded by One who entered human life by a miraculous birth and who left the human arena by a victory over the death which He voluntarily suffered for the sake of saving men.

The chief reason for the republication of this volume, originally printed under the title *Resurrection Realities,* is the current need for a positive presentation of Christian truth in the person of a living Lord. The book does not purport to be exhaustive in its scope; it is rather intended to be suggestive. Four of its chapters were given as addresses in the chapel of Wheaton College in pre-Easter services; the others have been delivered at other times or written anew. All of them spring from protracted meditation on the central theme of a living Christ.

Grateful acknowledgments are due to Dr. V. Raymond Edman, President of Wheaton College, for his contribution of the Foreword; to *The King's Business,* whose editor consented to the re-use of an article published in its pages several years ago; to Harper and Brothers, Publishers, for permission to quote from *The Rise of Gentile Christianity,* by F. J. Foakes-Jackson; to the Appleton-Century Company, for consent to quote from *Who Moved the Stone?* by Frank Morison; and

8 *Introduction*

to the International Council of Religious Education for the use of the American Revised Version in all quotations from the Bible that appear in this volume.

Special thanks are due to Professor John Lars Johnson of the University of Illinois and to Miss Mildred Cook of Los Angeles for their many helpful suggestions and corrections on the original manuscript, and to the author's wife, Helen J. Tenney, whose loyal encouragement aided greatly the production of the book, and to the Zondervan Publishing House for undertaking the task of reprinting to meet current popular request.

Wheaton, Illinois   MERRILL C. TENNEY
1964

Contents

CHAPTER I

The Central Verity of Faith

> For I delivered unto you first of all that which also I received: that Christ died for our sins according to the scriptures; and that he was buried; and that he hath been raised on the third day according to the scriptures; and that he appeared. . . .
>
> I Corinthians 15:3–5

ALL evangelical Christians, whatever the age in which they have lived and whatever the peculiar doctrinal emphases they may have held, have generally agreed on certain truths which they have regarded as necessary to an acceptable Christian faith.

The existence of a personal, self-revealing God, the incarnation of that God in the person of His Son, Jesus Christ, who was born of the Virgin Mary, the manifestation of that Son in His vicarious death upon the cross of Calvary which affords forgiveness of sins to believers, His bodily resurrection, His ascension, His triumphal return, salvation by faith in Him, and the necessity for personal holiness in living—these fundamental beliefs are like the stones of an arch which support the superstructure of historical theology that goes by the name of Christianity.

Yet this structure of belief which is held by common consent is under severe attack. Like an army which keeps its front unbroken by vigorously defending its key position, we can defend our faith best by emphasizing our key position. In order to do so, we need to know what the key position is. Which of these doctrines is the most important? Which is the foundation and also the proof of all the others?

This passage in I Corinthians was written as an apology for Christianity. The rationalists of Corinth had said that the supernatural was impossible. In denying the resurrection they had felt that they had merely removed an excrescence from Christian faith; they did not realize that by so doing they had severed its jugular vein.

The most important doctrine of our Christian faith is not the virgin birth with its tender and sacred mystery, nor the atonement on Calvary where the blood was shed that brought the love and forgiveness of God to a ruined world, but the physical resurrection of Jesus Christ from the dead. Without the resurrection the virgin birth would be incredible, for why should we accept a biological miracle as the origin of a life which was swallowed up hopelessly in death? Without the resurrection there would be no atonement, for the value of Christ's death as an atonement depends upon the quality of the one who died. If, like all other men, He succumbed to death and never triumphed over it, His death might have been that of a martyr or a hero; but it could never have been the means of bringing salvation to others. The resurrection singles Him out as different from others and gives a different value to all the other facts of His life.

This importance of the resurrection as a factual basis for faith was clearly understood by the first preachers of the Christian church. In thirteen sermons in the book of Acts which are addressed to unbelievers, eight stress the resurrection as the cardinal doctrine and the incontrovertible proof of faith. In three others it is implied, as in Paul's address to the multitude in Acts 22, where he claims that he conversed with the Risen Christ. In the two remaining instances where the resurrection is neither expressed nor implied, the circumstances of the moment brought other matters to the forefront, as in the case of the colloquy of Philip and the eunuch (Acts 8:26–38). Even here the absence of reference to the resurrection does not mean that Philip did not mention it; for the text merely gives the point of departure in his discourse, and summarizes the rest by saying, "And beginning from this scripture, preached unto him Jesus." The two most important addresses in Acts which are represented as complete units rather than as fragments of speeches, Peter's sermon at Pentecost (Acts 2) and Paul's address in the synagogue at Antioch of Pisidia (Acts 13:16–41), are built directly upon the resurrection and devote a large part of their argument to it. In the fifteenth chapter of I Corinthians Paul replied to the challenge of those who did not believe in a resurrection of any kind. In his counterargument we find his statement that the resurrection was foremost among the facts upon which the structure of Christianity was built, and that he accorded to it a place of primacy in his preaching.

The reason for this primacy is not hard to seek. Christianity, as the late Dr. J. Gresham Machen once remarked, is not built on a complex of ideas but on an historic fact. If our faith is merely the more or less coherent philosophical scheme which some well-meaning thinker has evolved, it is bound to be superseded in time by some other scheme produced by some better thinker, or else it can be challenged as being merely the belief of one group of people who are no better or worse than any other group. As a world view it takes its place with all other world views, which are the results of human attempts to formulate some method of systematizing and overcoming the world in which we find ourselves. But Christianity is more than a world view; it is the account of the intervention of the supernatural personal God into the affairs of men in a definite event of history. The resurrection is that point at which the supernatural life of God became tangent to the ordinary life of man in the space-time continuum and manifested itself so convincingly that its reality and power can never be gainsaid or denied.

Such a tremendous assertion as this needs substantiation. If it be true, then the resurrection is the most important fact of all history as well as being the cornerstone of Christian faith. What proofs can be adduced to show that the story of the resurrection of Christ from the grave is not simply an idle legend or a deliberate invention for the purpose of propagating a cult? In answer, we present five distinct testimonies to its verity.

1. THE TESTIMONY OF DOCUMENTARY RECORD

The only records that we have of the life of Jesus of Nazareth that afford any clear picture of His career are the four canonical Gospels of Matthew, Mark, Luke, and John. The apocryphal Gospels which purport to give information concerning His life are generally conceded to have been drawn from these, and to be much less reliable in content. These four date from earliest Christian times and were undoubtedly written before the close of the first century; in fact, they were probably written within the lifetime of men who had seen Jesus personally. They were generally received as reliable by those who first read them, and there is no good reason for doubting the essential accuracy of their statements.

Furthermore, in their discussion of the life of Jesus they are singularly free from the fanciful embroidery of hero-worship which characterizes much of the literature of antiquity. Even a hasty comparison of the canonical Gospels with the apocryphal Gospels will show how extravagant and overdrawn are the latter. The marvel is not that the Gospels contain so many miracles and make so many claims for Jesus; the marvel is that they present so few. In consideration of the fact that they were first written and used in a group of people who worshiped Jesus as God (on the testimony of Pliny, a pagan Roman), the wonder is that the Gospels did not embellish his memory with more marvels than have been recorded. They offer relatively little in the way of comment and interpretation; they relate some of Christ's utterances and acts, and leave the reader to draw his own conclusions.

All four of these Gospels agree on the fact of the resurrection. Whatever disagreements there may be in small details, all agree on the great facts that Jesus died; that He was buried; that the tomb was found empty on the morning of the third day, the first day of the week; and that He subsequently appeared to His disciples. On these matters they give a united testimony.

Nor are the minor disagreements necessarily indicative of falsehood. If four witnesses all appeared in a court case and all told exactly the same story in exactly the same words, the judge would suspect criminal collaboration between the witnesses, and would have every right to do so. No two witnesses of a given event will give identical testimony, especially when they are under nervous pressure and are surprised out of their wits by what they witness.

Once the author was taking a class in historiography. One

day the professor came into class with a handful of papers which he proceeded to distribute to the class. He then said that he had given each student a set of papers in which were copied the original sources of some historical event. He instructed the class to analyze what the witnesses said, and to write an account of exactly what happened. On one set were written five different accounts of the battle of Lexington and Concord which appeared in the diaries or writings of eyewitnesses who were present at that fateful skirmish of April 19, 1775. No two of them agreed in any detail, and some of them seemed to be diametrically opposed to one another in the facts that they asserted. Would it have been fair to conclude that because the witnesses did not agree perfectly the battle never took place? That would have been absurd, of course; for it did, and tangible evidences of it survive unto this day. One could only conclude that while some of the details could not easily be accounted for, the main fact was clear: the actuality and issue of the battle were without question.

So it is with the resurrection. Some of the details are hard to fit into the framework of the sequence of events, but the significant fact of the empty tomb, acknowledged by friends and foes alike, and the subsequent appearance of the living Lord, attested by all the documents, cannot be denied.

2. THE TESTIMONY OF LIVING WITNESSES

If it be objected that documents can be forged, we can turn to another source: the presence of living witnesses. In I Corinthians 15, written by Paul about A.D. 54, we have a list of persons who were living in his time, and who, he says, could testify to the actuality of the resurrection. The genuineness of this Epistle has never been successfully challenged; and as written evidence it antedates, probably, the earliest of the Gospels, or is at least contemporaneous with it. In this passage Paul mentions five persons or groups to whom he appeals as witnesses.

1 The first is "Cephas." This person appears to be identical with Peter, for Cephas is merely the Aramaic name of which Peter is the Greek equivalent. Of all the apostles, Peter was one of the most intimate with Jesus, and certainly would have recognized Him or would have been able to detect any fraudulent impersonation of Him. Paul asserts that Jesus "appeared" to Cephas. Surely if somebody else had endeavored to impersonate Jesus after His death, and to create the illusion that He had risen, this loyal and intimate follower would have been able to penetrate the disguise. Yet nothing of the sort took place. This Peter staked his life and ministry on the fact that Jesus had risen, and is recorded as saying, "Who ate and drank with him after he rose from the dead" (Acts 10:41).

2 The second witness is the group of "the Twelve." That phrase, "the Twelve," is probably to be taken as a loose collective rather than as an exact number, since Judas Iscariot was not with them after the resurrection. If it be possible that one man could be mistaken in his witness, it is certainly less so that eleven could be. Had they been expecting Christ to rise, even if He had not, we might feel that they worked themselves into the emotional state in which they would think that He had risen; and that the resurrection was merely the result of wishful thinking. On the contrary, there is no inkling in the accounts of this group that they really did expect Jesus to rise. The dominant emotion in the days after the crucifixion was not expectation but fear, which the very appearance of Jesus deepened.

The sudden deliverance of these men from their fears and the transformation of the cowering little company into a fearless cordon of preachers indicates that something happened to produce that transformation.

③ The third witness is a group of above five hundred brethren who were together. Abraham Lincoln once said, "You can fool some of the people all the time, and all the people some of the time, but you cannot fool all the people all the time." To create an illusion that would fool five hundred people simultaneously and so successfully that twenty-five years later they would be willing to affirm in the face of all odds that Jesus had risen, would in itself be something of a miracle.

④ The fourth witness is James. James was the Lord's brother. The Gospel of John tells us that he and the other brethren of the Lord did not believe on Him while He was engaged in His public ministry. Though our friends may be truthful, their testimony concerning our virtues is not so reliable as the testimony of our enemies. If our friends compliment us, their judgment may be warped unconsciously by their friendship; but if our enemies say anything good about us, or acknowledge our claims, the probability is that their testimony is true. James was living when this Epistle was written; and his testimony that Jesus had risen from the dead is all the more convincing because he had not been a partisan of His, but rather an opponent. The apocryphal *Gospel According to the Hebrews* narrates how Jesus appeared to James and announced His own resurrection, and how James believed. Irrespective of the reliability of this document, it at least indicated that tradition ascribed the conversion of James to Jesus' appearance to him.

⑤ The last witness is Paul himself. He claims that Christ appeared to him as to one "born out of due time." Doubtless this allusion is to his experience on the Damascus Road, when he was converted. The radical transformation of purpose and character that took place in this man at that time demands an adequate explanation. This brilliant young pupil of Gamaliel, thoroughly trained in Judaism and regarding the followers of the Nazarene as being the duped victims of a crucified impostor, was not only satisfied with his status before God, but was also zealous to the point of fanaticism in exterminating his opponents. How does it happen, then, that he suddenly espouses the faith which he had set out to extinguish? If we are to place any credence in his own words, we shall have to accept his explanation for this remarkable psychological phenomenon, and admit that the appearance of the Risen Christ produced this change in him.

It is clear, then, that before the written documents of the Gospels there were numerous witnesses who, from differing viewpoints and for differing reasons, agreed in their testimony that Jesus Christ had risen from the dead; and that their testimony was inextricably bound up with the subsequent conduct of their lives as well as being the content of their united witness.

3. THE TESTIMONY OF MARTYRS

Testimony is of no higher value than the character of the witness. How valid were these witnesses? Testimony to the resurrection cost these men something. The very records which contain their witness tell us that they endured all kinds of privations for the faith which the resurrection had engendered. Stoning, flogging, imprisonment, ostracism, banishment, confiscation of their goods—maltreatment of every kind was their lot. Nor was this merely the passive effect of their preaching, an outcome which they did not expect and from which they fled; they actually courted it and defied the authorities of their day for the sake of proclaiming what they believed.

But, it may be objected, these men, like others, were fanatics; and fanatics can be found to support any cause, whether it has foundation in fact or not. Quite so, but while men will die for a falsehood which they believe to be true, they will not die for what they know to be false. If Jesus never rose from the dead, these men had ample opportunity to know the truth. Seven weeks after His body was taken down from the cross they were boldly preaching in the city of Jerusalem that He had risen, and they were staking life, liberty, and reputation on that proposition. There is not in the record of history the slightest suggestion that His enemies ever produced His body, or that they had any concrete evidence to prove that it was still in the tomb. If His friends removed it, not a scintilla of rumor to that effect disturbed the preaching of those who had been His most intimate followers. When they preached the resurrection, they had everything to lose and nothing to gain by dishonesty. To believe that they deliberately preached what they knew to be a lie, or that they sacrificed their reputations, their standing with their countrymen, and their liberties—all for an uncertainty—makes a bigger demand on our credulity than to accept as fact their main assertion that He had risen.

4. THE TESTIMONY OF THE ORIGIN OF THE CHURCH

Whatever be one's attitude on the question as to whether Christ rose bodily from the dead, the existence of the Christian church is acknowledged by all. Historians, agnostic or Christian, are compelled to admit that for a period of nineteen hundred years the church has been a powerful factor in the social, economic, political, and religious affairs of the world. Every movement of this type must have an origin. Mohammedanism can be traced to the personal influence and teachings of Mohammed. Buddhism originated with the teachings of Siddartha Gautama. In every case which can be cited as in any way parallel to Christianity, the testimony of the movement concerning itself is given serious consideration in accounting for its rise. How can we deal fairly with Christianity if we do otherwise? If this movement, patent to all, claims to have its origin in the resurrection of Christ, then we must find some other cause adequate to account for it if we repudiate the resurrection.

Even historians who do not believe in the resurrection of Christ have acknowledged this fact. F. J. Foakes-Jackson, a man who does not believe in the bodily resurrection of Christ, but whose scholarship cannot be questioned, says in his book on *The Rise of Gentile Christianity,*

> That after Jesus was put to death He rose from the grave may be questioned, but all must assent to the proposition that His immediate followers believed that He had done so; and before the earliest Christian writings had appeared this was the accepted belief of the community. Indeed, without a belief in the Resurrection, Christianity as a religion would never have begun to exist.

What caused that belief? The men who preached the resurrection were not accustomed to dealing in psychological subtleties nor in philosophical daydreams. There must have been something compelling in their experience to make them assert so revolutionary a doctrine as this. If we grant once and for all the simple fact of the resurrection, all else becomes clear. If not, we are left with a permanent puzzle on our hands. Why is it more reasonable to adopt the uncertainty of denial of the resurrection in the place of the certainty of its occurrence, even though the latter may presuppose a fact that lies outside of our immediate experience?

5. THE TESTIMONY OF THE UNWILLING

Were the fact of the resurrection defended only by those who are inclined to believe in it by training or by emotional predisposition, we might ascribe it to wishful thinking. When those who are opposed to it by training and inclination are compelled to acknowledge its verity we have even more reason to believe in it.

Not very many years ago a man who wrote under the name of Frank Morison produced a book entitled *Who Moved the Stone?* in which he treated analytically the last week of the life of Jesus. He began the study with the avowed purpose of destroying the delusion of belief in the resurrection, and he expected that a careful scrutiny of the evidence would prove the belief to be unfounded. Although he proceeded on purely rationalistic grounds without the assumption of inspiration, the sheer weight of the evidence of the Gospels drove him to conclusions opposite to the aims with which he started. After a searching examination of all the facts, he concluded with this statement:

> There may be, and as the writer thinks, there certainly is, a profoundly historical basis for that much disputed sentence in the Apostles' Creed—"the *third day* He rose again from the dead."

This testimony could be duplicated by that of Gilbert West of the eighteenth century, and of others. If, then, men hostile to Christian faith have been forced to a belief in this apparently most unbelievable of miracles, how can anyone say that our faith is merely the result of gullibility?

Granting, then, that the resurrection is a fact, what of it? Certain corollaries follow from it as surely as day follows dawn.

Firstly, if Jesus Christ rose from the tomb alive on the morning of the first day of the week, He is a living person today. We are not merely cherishing the idealized memory of One who died the death of a hero nineteen centuries ago, nor are we worshiping the personified complex of a doctrinal system. He is living today, and His work in the world is still going on. Though invisible He is not unreal, but still molds human personality and still guides and teaches, though not present with us here in corporeal form.

Secondly, by the resurrection He is proclaimed different from all other men. Others have lived good lives; but their virtues have not been openly acknowledged in resurrection as pleasing to God. Other men have died heroically; but their heroism was tragedy because it was swallowed up in the grave. Others have promised great things, but have not lived to make good their promises. But of Christ it could be said: "Who was declared to be the Son of God with power, according to the spirit of holiness, by the resurrection from the dead" (Rom. 1:4). His eternal supremacy over all others is established by this one great triumph.

Lastly, we must deal with Him as with a living person. We are not challenged to give our allegiance to the ideal of a person who has faded away on the horizon of history. We do not seek forgiveness of sins from a legal proposition. We do not serve a movement or an organization. We shall not face a set of ethical principles at the judgment. "Lovest thou ME?" was the question of the Risen Christ to a wavering disciple. It is a personal call to allegiance. "If we confess our sins, HE [not it] is faithful and righteous to forgive us our sins" (I John 1:9). "What wilt THOU have me to do?" not "How can I do something in the Church?" is the question of the new convert. "He [God] hath appointed a day in which he will judge the world in righteousness by the man whom he hath ordained; whereof he hath given assurance unto all men, in that he hath raised him from the dead" (Acts 17:31) is the certain prospect for the future. From the empty grave in Joseph's garden, the most stupendous and best attested fact of history, comes the dynamic faith in Christ risen, which is the vital heart of Christianity and the everlasting hope of a death-ridden world.

CHAPTER II

The Prophetic Forecast

The Christ should suffer, and rise again from the dead the third day.

Luke 24:46

ON THE first day of the week after the crucifixion two travelers were wearily plodding along the road from Jerusalem to Emmaus. The afternoon sun was hot, and they were tired. So startling had been the turn of affairs in the previous week and so strained were their emotions that they scarcely noticed the stranger who joined their company and walked along with them. When he inquired about the subject of their conversation they halted, amazed that he should be ignorant of the events which had just taken place in Jerusalem.

Since he seemed sympathetic, they poured out their hearts to him. They recalled that Jesus of Nazareth had been their friend and leader. He had been a prophet whose deeds had been acclaimed by all the people, but the rulers had delivered Him up to death and had crucified Him. All the bitterness of their disappointment and the hopelessness of their attitude was bound up in these words: "We hoped that it was he who should redeem Israel" (Luke 24:21). They had cherished the hope that He might be the Messiah, the Deliverer who should bring spiritual and political emancipation to their nation, but the cross had ended all that. How could a crucified prophet effect any de-

liverance? And more, how could He fit the picture of the prophets who had spoken of His ruling the nations with a rod of iron
and dashing them in pieces like a potter's vessel? His end had
been so incongruous with the prophetic picture that they could
only feel that they had been mistaken.

They admitted, of course, that some of the women who went
to the tomb had returned, reporting that they had seen a vision
of angels who said that He was alive. Their estimate of this
testimony is eloquently stated in the terse words, "But *Him*
(italics ours) they saw not." Something more than second-hand
evidence of Christ's resurrection was necessary to convince these
men who knew that He had died, and who were confident that
His end precluded His being the expected fulfillment of the
Messianic promises.

The stranger did not share their viewpoint, but rebuked them
sharply.

> O foolish men, and slow of heart to believe in all that the
> prophets have spoken! Behooved it not the Christ to suffer
> these things, and to enter into his glory?
>
> (Luke 24:25, 26)

Then, beginning with Moses and continuing through all the
prophets, He explained to them all the things in Scripture that
were a prediction of Himself. That this explanation included
a discussion of the resurrection is made plain by the declaration
of the Lord Jesus on a subsequent occasion:

> And he said unto them, These are my words which I spake
> unto you, while I was yet with you, that all things must needs
> be fulfilled, which are written in the law of Moses, and the
> prophets, and the psalms, concerning me. Then opened he
> their mind, that they might understand the scriptures; and he

said unto them, Thus it is written, that the Christ should suffer, and rise again from the dead the third day . . .

(Luke 24:44–46)

The error of these men which led to their hopelessness lay in an incomplete understanding of the prophetic scriptures. They had seen only the fact that the Messiah must come in glory: they had missed entirely the prediction of the suffering and of the resurrection. The discourse of the Lord Jesus on this occasion was designed to set their minds at rest by showing them that the disturbing occurrences which had destroyed their confidence in Him as Messiah were really the exact fulfillment of the prophetic word.

The text of Jesus' exposition of the scriptures on this occasion has not been preserved for us, and we are left to surmise as best we can what passages in the Old Testament were employed as predictive of the resurrection. The Jewish scriptures contain comparatively little direct reference to any such phenomenon, and the application of typical situations as teaching it is uncertain at best. Yet the Lord Jesus has by the use of the term "the Christ" definitely connected the prophecies of the resurrection with Messianic prophecy. We may expect to find at least some hint of the resurrection in the general line of prophecy concerning the Coming One. Furthermore, it is quite probable that the instruction of the "forty days" was reflected in the later teaching of the apostles. If that be so, the Messianic prophecies of the Old Testament in conjunction with the Messianic sermons of the New Testament should give us a key to the place of the resurrection in Old Testament prophecy.

Such *a priori* reasoning is not always sound, for experience teaches that many things which, theoretically, ought to be true are not true practically. On the other hand, we know that Jesus during His life taught the necessity of the resurrection. When the Sadducees objected to the doctrine on the basis of inferential interpretation of the Law, He said, "Ye do err, not knowing the scriptures, nor the power of God" (Matt. 22:29). If He taught the resurrection on the basis of the scriptures, that doctrine must have been in the Word, and we are justified in seeking to identify the prophecies by their counterparts in the teaching of the New Testament.

What are these passages?

The first Messianic prophecy of which we have record is the Protevangelium in Genesis 3:15:

> And I will put enmity between thee and the woman, and between thy seed and her seed: he shall bruise thy head, and thou shalt bruise his heel.

The figure is that of an Oriental gardener, who, seeing a venomous serpent in the pathway, crushes its head, but receives its venom in his heel. There are certain implications in this text which may have a bearing on the resurrection.

Firstly, this promise was spoken for the benefit of a man who was under sentence of death for sin. "In the day that thou eatest thereof thou shalt surely die." In the crushing of the head of the serpent, deliverance was promised; and in order to effect that deliverance, the Redeemer had to be able to conquer death.

Secondly, the man received the venom of the serpent and yet lived to triumph over it. How could Christ take upon Himself the consequence of the serpent's sting and yet live? Resurrection seems to be the answer.

In the episode of Isaac and Abraham on Mt. Moriah as given

in Genesis 22 there is depicted the death of the Seed and His subsequent restoration. Of course, Isaac did not die actually, only potentially. Nevertheless, it is interesting to note that he was the representation of the Messiah, the Chosen Seed, and that the author of Hebrews says that God raised him "from the dead; from whence he [Abraham] did also in a figure receive him back" (Heb. 11:19). This passage is not applied specifically to Christ by any of the New Testament writers, though the parallelism is striking.

There is no further clear-cut statement in the stream of Messianic prophecy until we come to the symbolism of the Jewish ceremonies as recorded in the later books of the Pentateuch. In Leviticus 23, three feasts are described as "set feasts of Jehovah." The first, the Passover, speaks of vicarious sacrifice and of separation from sin. The third, the Presentation of the Wave-Loaves, is the Feast of Pentecost. Between these two is the Feast of the Firstfruits. This feast was held on the third day after the Passover, fifty days before Pentecost. The first fruits of the barley harvest were presented as the first sign of returning life after the burial of the seed, and the feast was accompanied by the presentation of a sacrifice (Lev. 23:9–14).

Compare this record with the resurrection. The resurrection took place on the third day after the death of the Passover sacrifice, and fifty days before Pentecost. It was the harbinger and symbol of new life from the dead. The Lord Jesus applied the figure to Himself when He said, "Except a grain of wheat fall into the earth and die, it abideth by itself alone; but if it die, it beareth much fruit" (John 12:24). Paul used the same figure when he declared, "But now hath Christ been raised from the dead, the firstfruits of them that are asleep" (I Cor. 15:20).

Perhaps his utterance owed its symbolism to knowledge of Jesus' interpretation of the Old Testament passage. As the natural harvest bespoke the power of an irresistible life which the damp and mold of the ground could not permanently restrain, so the resurrection of Christ demonstrated the power of the divine life over all the restraints of the grave. The Messiah must demonstrate that power in order to prove His Messiahship.

With the passing of the theocracy and the inception of the kingdom, prophecy became an increasingly important factor in the life of Israel. Among the first of her seers was the royal prophet David. The sixteenth psalm records David's spiritual aspiration. He coveted the "goodly heritage" and "pleasant places," and more than that, he sought a continuation in the life to come. His words go beyond his own aspirations, as he asserts boldly:

> For thou wilt not leave my soul to Sheol;
> Neither wilt thou suffer thy holy one to see corruption.
> Thou wilt show me the path of life:
> In thy presence is fulness of joy;
> In thy right hand there are pleasures for evermore.
>
> (Psa. 16:10, 11)

Sheol to the Jew was not primarily a place of punishment, but was merely the place of departed spirits, whether good or evil. Jacob regarded Sheol as his destiny (Gen. 37:35). Since Sheol was considered by the Jews as the common lot of all souls after death, this prophecy has a surprising note. It speaks of deliverance from death and of an exaltation after death. The soul was not to remain in the realm of the shadow, nor the body to fester in the corruption of the grave. Deliverance is part of the psalmist's faith.

The New Testament, however, restricts the utterance of Psalm 16 to the resurrection of Christ. Both Peter and Paul (Acts 2:25–31, 13:35) interpret the passage as David's prediction of the resurrection of the Messiah. The prediction was fulfilled by the Lord Jesus, as the writers of the New Testament unhesitatingly declare.

Other psalms of the period later than David's kingdom echo this hope. Psalm 49:15 declares, "God will redeem my soul from the power of Sheol; for he will receive me." Psalm 73:24, a psalm of Asaph, says, "Thou wilt guide me with thy counsel, and afterward receive me to glory." These passages lack the exactness of the pronouncement in Psalm 16, but strengthen the concept of the resurrection in the Psalms.

Among the writings of the prophets there are several allusions to this topic. Hosea 6:1, 2 represents the nation of Israel as saying:

> Come, and let us return unto Jehovah; for he hath torn, and he will heal us; he hath smitten, and he will bind us up. After two days will he revive us: on the third day he will raise us up, and we shall live before him.

Not too much stress can be put on this passage because (1) it applies primarily to the nation of Israel, not to an individual; (2) its application is to restoration from sin rather than to resurrection from death; (3) it is not quoted directly in the New Testament as a prediction of the resurrection. On the other hand, Hosea 11:1, though obviously applying to the nation, is used in Matthew 2:15 as a prediction concerning the Messiah, and the phrase "on the third day" is used only here in the Old Testament in direct reference to resurrection. If Hosea 11:1 is a prophecy of Christ given indirectly, so may this be.

Strong implications of resurrection occur in the Servant prophecies of Isaiah. The Messianic use of these prophecies is abundantly confirmed by the New Testament, which applies them directly to Christ. In the first public address of the Lord Jesus in the synagogue at Nazareth He quoted Isaiah 61 (Lk. 4:16–19), and Philip expounded the fifty-third chapter of Isaiah to the eunuch as he "preached unto him Jesus" (Acts 8:26–35). In Isaiah 53, in the passage describing the death of the Servant, are these words:

> And they made his grave with the wicked, and with a rich man in his death; although he had done no violence, neither was any deceit in his mouth . . . when thou shalt make his soul an offering for sin, he shall see his seed, he shall prolong his days, and the pleasure of Jehovah shall prosper in his hand.
>
> (Isa. 53:9, 10)

According to this passage His grave is made; He dies, and is buried; yet "he shall see his seed, he shall prolong his days." How can this paradox be resolved? The answer is: Only on the basis of resurrection. The prophecy was fulfilled. The grave was made with the wicked, for doubtless the body of Jesus would have been thrown into the potter's field had not Joseph of Arimathea given it burial in his own tomb, where He was "with a rich man in his death." In the resurrection He came to life again, and saw His seed, prolonged His days, and the pleasure of God prospered in His hand.

The example of Jonah is cited by the Lord Jesus Himself as a figure of His resurrection. As the prophet remained in the great fish for three days and nights, so the Lord Himself was swallowed by death and finally given back. Jesus quoted this passage more as a sign or illustration than as a direct prediction, yet it stands as depicting His release from the jaws of death.

The last prophecy is in some ways the most spectacular of all. In Zechariah 12:10, where the prophet is describing the future Day of the Lord, he speaks for Jehovah as saying:

> And I will pour upon the house of David, and upon the inhabitants of Jerusalem, the spirit of grace and of supplication; and·they shall look unto me whom they have pierced; and they shall mourn for him, as one mourneth for his only son, and shall be in bitterness for him, as one that is in bitterness for his first-born.

This passage is quoted in John 19:37 as being directly prophetic of the crucifixion and death of Jesus. Yet Jehovah applies it to Himself on the day of final triumph, and asserts that Israel will mourn over having pierced the One who appears in glory. How can the One who died on Calvary's cross and who was buried in Joseph's garden reappear in glory unless a resurrection intervene? While this conclusion is merely inferential, it seems fair in the light of existing Scripture.

Thus the voices of prophecy in the Law and Psalms and Prophets, spoken over many centuries and in widely varying circumstances, unite in implying that the Risen Redeemer will remove the curse of death which rests upon the human race; that the Risen Firstfruits will be the harbinger of the greater harvest of the sons of God; that the Risen Holy One will satisfy our longing for eternal life; that the Risen Servant will make full expiation of our guilt and will bring to fulfillment the purpose of God; and that in the Risen King Jehovah shall reveal Himself to an astounded and penitent Israel.

> Come ye faithful, raise the strain
>   Of triumphant gladness.
> God has brought His Israel
>   Into joy from sadness;
> Loosed from Pharaoh's bitter yoke
>   Jacob's sons and daughters,
> Led them with unmoistened foot
>   Through the Red Sea waters.
>
> 'Tis the spring of souls today,
>   Christ hath burst His prison
> And from three days' sleep in death
>   As a sun hath risen;
> All the winter of our sins
>   Long and dark, is flying
> From His light, to whom we give
>   Laud and praise undying.
>   (John of Damascus)

CHAPTER III

The Basis of Belief

> And if Christ hath not been raised, your faith is vain; ye are yet in your sins.
>
> I Corinthians 15:17

ONE fine summer day a man was lying idly on his back in an English apple orchard watching the clouds sail by. An apple fell off one of the near-by trees, and narrowly missed hitting his nose. Such an occurrence certainly could not be called extraordinary; for apples had been falling from trees for millenniums before this person was born. In this case, however, the fall of the apple was a bit extraordinary, because it was the starting point from which Sir Isaac Newton formulated several great laws of physics which we recognize today as part of the basis of our understanding of the physical world. The fact of the falling fruit was not unusual; but Newton's keen mind saw that there was something behind the fact, and by careful analysis of the principles involved he brought out the significance of it.

Granting that the resurrection is a fact far more significant than that which prompted the formulation of the laws of physics, we must seek its meaning. Facts do not just happen; they bespeak principles, powers, or forces behind them. If so remarkable an event as the resurrection of Christ actually did take place, it must mean that behind the occurrence there is the operation of a new force in the world of which previously there had been little or no evidence. Furthermore, if we are to interpret it fairly, we must do so in the light of the record and of the teaching which sprang from it. Since it is inextricably bound up with the person of Jesus, it must have a significance connected with Him.

Paul tells us that the fact of the resurrection calls for faith in the person of Christ. Certainly any man who so rose should be regarded as different from the rank and file of humanity. If he is different from all other men, and above them in that He has conquered death, then He has the right to leadership and a claim on our highest allegiance. How does the resurrection challenge our faith?

1. FAITH IN HIS PROMISE

The world has had many men as leaders who have made promises, some of which have been fulfilled and some of which have gone unfulfilled. When Jesus first appeared, teaching, preaching, and performing miracles of healing, the leaders of His nation were suspicious of Him. What right had He to assume the leadership of the multitude? Jealousy of His popularity compelled them to question Him for His credentials.

In reply, He gave only one answer. "Destroy this temple," He said, "and in three days I will raise it up" (John 2:19). (Of course His enemies misunderstood Him. They thought that He spoke of the temple that crowned the hills of Jerusalem, whereas He was speaking of the temple of His body.)

On another occasion, when they asked Him for a sign, He replied: "An evil and adulterous generation seeketh after a sign; and there shall no sign be given to it but the sign of Jonah the prophet: for as Jonah was three days and three nights in the belly of the whale; so shall the Son of man be three days and three nights in the heart of the earth" (Matt. 12:39, 40). On both of these occasions He made His resurrection His chief credential and promised unconditionally that He would rise again from the dead.

If He had defaulted on this phenominal promise, we would immediately lose faith in Him. Had it been a conditional prediction of no special importance and had He failed to make it good, it might reasonably be supposed that the conditions were not met; but when He twice asserted that He regarded this event as being the supreme proof and sign of His mission, we can say that faith in all His promises is grounded on the reality of this particular event.

The importance of this credential has been generally recognized by the unbelieving world. During the period of the Enlightenment in France a man came to Talleyrand, the cynical and atheistic Prime Minister, told him that he had a new religion to propagate and asked for the Prime Minister's endorsement. When he inquired how he could obtain popular support for his new cult, Talleyrand is reported to have said: "I advise you, sir, to get yourself crucified, and to rise on the third day." If he could do that, his success would be assured. Obviously, he could not; and his cult has been long since forgotten. Jesus did die and did rise again; and His promises are all good because He lives.

2. FAITH IN HIS PERSON

If Jesus actually rose from the dead, He is thereby differentiated from all other men. True, others had been brought back from death; but as far as the record goes, none of them had ever exercised the powers after death that Jesus did, nor did they ever claim that they would take their lives again by their own power. None of them had ever predicted his own resurrection. As far as their personal expectation was concerned, the resurrection from death was not an integral or predictable part of their careers. In Jesus' case it was. He spoke of death and resurrection as calmly and confidently as if He had been talking about a planned visit to the house of a friend.

There were many prophets of the Old Testament who left a longer record of preaching than did Jesus, and who, on a quantitative basis, might have been reckoned of at least equal importance to Him in the history of Judaism. Some of them performed miracles as spectacular as those which He performed. The multitude continually asked Him whether He were "Elijah" or "that prophet." Why should He be singled out as an exception in the great succession of the prophets of Israel?

The answer lies in the words of His own disciples. They too were familiar with the prophets, and doubtless knew their words and significance as well as we of the modern day. Living in the land where the prophets had flourished, and in a civilization which had changed less since the days of the prophets than has ours in the last century, they would be able to make a very fair assessment of the claims of Jesus in comparison with the claims of all those who had preceded Him. Nor were they inclined to believe that He would climax His career differently from those prophets who had suffered martyrdom; for in spite of His predictions, they seemed to have no anticipation whatsoever that He would rise from the dead. Yet when Thomas, the least credulous and the most pessimistic of the group, beheld Jesus after the resurrection, and realized that He was actually living, he exclaimed, "My Lord and my God!" This utterance is inexplicable in the mouth of a Jew, unless he was convinced that in Jesus of Nazareth Deity was resident as it was not in the prophets. Christ is, in the words of Paul, "declared to be the Son of God with power, according to the spirit of holiness, by the resurrection from the dead" (Rom. 1:4). It was impossible that He should be held by death, for on Him death could place no claims. Deity cannot be imprisoned in dust.

3. FAITH IN HIS PURPOSE

The earthly life of Jesus, short as it was, was geared to a purpose. This purpose He declared to His disciples shortly after the Great Confession which established firmly their attitude to Him as the Messiah and Son of God. "From that time began Jesus to show unto his disciples, that he must go unto Jerusalem, and suffer many things of the elders and chief priests and scribes, and be killed, and the third day be raised up" (Matt. 16:21). His language makes clear that His death and resurrection were the main goal of His career. The same impression is conveyed by the very structure of the Gospels, for the last week of His life is given about one third of the space in their accounts. "The Son of man also came not to be ministered unto, but to minister, and to give his life a ransom for many" (Mk. 10:45).

He taught that His death would have a distinct effect on the destinies of men. Yet why should His death have any moral value for men greater than the death of any other religious teacher? Could it not be said of Socrates, for instance, that he gave his life in the cause of human advancement, and as a benefit to the youth of Athens? If Jesus merely died, His death may have been the death of a martyr, or the tragic end of a prophet who was ahead of his time; but it could not have been the atoning death of a Savior of sinners. The atonement is based on the value of the One who died rather than upon the fact of death; and the uniqueness of His person as evinced by the resurrection proves that this death was more than merely an heroic gesture. He "was delivered up for our trespasses, and was raised for our justification" (Rom. 4:25).

4. FAITH IN HIS PREEMINENCE

If He is still living, how shall we evaluate Him? If by His death and resurrection He is the Savior of men and the key to all our destinies, where shall we place Him?

He must be the center of our thinking. For centuries men have sought the answer to the riddle of the universe. Whence did we come? Why are we here? Whither are we going? Here is One who had the answers to these questions. He knew that He came from God, that He came to do the will of God, and that He was going to God. He taught men that they were the creation of God, that they were made for His service, and that they could share in the place which He went to prepare for them. All the keys to our life hang at His girdle, and in relation to Him we find our true place in this bewildering world. He deserves the first place in our philosophy of life; for He is "the firstborn from the dead; that in all things he might have the preeminence" (Col. 1:18).

He must be the center of our living. It may seem strange to make one person the model for all our conduct and the standard for all our ethics; yet such is God's decree. "He hath appointed a day in which he will judge the world in righteousness by the man whom he hath ordained; whereof he hath given assurance unto all men, in that he hath raised him from the dead" (Acts 17:31). The resurrection demonstrated God's approval of Him as the standard for all life, and by Him we shall be judged—measured—at the judgment seat of God.

By the resurrection, then, Jesus Christ is set apart from all other leaders of men. They had much to say of God and duty, of the world without and of the world within. Their words, wise and valuable as many of them were, have not solved for us the mysteries of life. But while men argued, He acted. While they debated the meaning of life, He demonstrated it. While they reasoned about the possibility of immortality, He rose from the dead. He has given us a sure basis for faith: "Because I live, ye shall live also" (John 14:19).

The issue is squarely before us as to what we shall do with this stupendous fact. Our attitude must be that of faith or else of unbelief; there can be no other alternative. On this choice hangs our destiny, for the Word of God says: "If thou shalt confess with thy mouth Jesus as Lord, and shalt believe in thy heart that God raised him from the dead, thou shalt be saved: for with the heart man believeth unto righteousness; and with the mouth confession is made unto salvation" (Rom. 10:9, 10). Build your faith today upon Him who died for our sins, Who lives to intercede for us and to sustain us, and Who will come again to receive us unto Himself.

CHAPTER IV

The Heritage of Liberty

For the law of the Spirit of life in Christ Jesus made me free from the law of sin and of death.

Romans 8:2

THE resurrection of Jesus Christ from the dead, spectacular though it was in its physical manifestation, was only the demonstration of what the divine power could do when applied to human need. Physical death, with its accompanying combination of weakness, futility, and corruption, is the consequence and picture of spiritual death. This principle is frequently stated in the Scriptures. "In the day that thou eatest thereof thou shalt surely die" (Gen. 2:17). "The soul that sinneth, it shall die" (Ezek. 18:20). "The wages of sin is death" (Rom. 6:23). "Sin, when it is fullgrown, bringeth forth death" (Jas. 1:15). These and many other passages state or illustrate the fact that physical death is only part of the more inclusive consequence of spiritual death that ensues when man by sin is separated from God.

This death is bondage. "Every one that committeth sin is the bondservant of sin," said Jesus (John 8:34). Every sin that we commit enthralls us more deeply than the one before. Tell one lie, and another must be told to cover the first. Indulge one lust, and it will demand increasing gratification until its victim is hopelessly bound by the habit. Do one wrong, and a host of fears and conflicts will follow. The man who sins finds that his freedom is illusory. He may not be in the toils of the law, but he stands condemned by his own conscience, and his fears and habits harass him and rob him of his peace of mind.

As the resurrection of Jesus depicted a victory over death, so the resurrection life of Christ imparted to the believer brings victory over sin. In the eighth chapter of Romans Paul gives an unsurpassed exposition of the resurrection principle as the basis of the Christian life. After showing in Chapter 7 that the righteousness of legality is insufficient to cope with the inner division and secret lusts of the heart, he depicts the new freedom which the resurrection power can bring. He discusses this liberty in three aspects.

1. FREEDOM FROM CONDEMNATION OF SIN

> There is therefore now no condemnation to them that are in Christ Jesus.
>
> (Rom. 8:1)

In the preceding passage he has pointed out that though a man may be righteous outwardly, he is inwardly a slave to the law of sin. To some degree he can control the expression of his impulses, but he cannot control the inner motions of a wicked heart. What is more, the law of God which is admittedly "holy, just, and good," has prompted these desires to sin. It is significant that the one commandment which he cites as producing the result is not the prohibition of murder or adultery or theft, but of covetousness, which is an inward matter. Murder is visible; covetousness is not.

Sin, then, is essentially not some particular act that one commits, but an inner motive that is part of him and that places him under condemnation. The stream of action is fouled at its source, and God has already pronounced sentence upon it. "I am carnal, sold under sin" (Rom. 7:14). Motives and intents are no longer wholly good; they may seem to be good, while hiding ulterior evil, or they may be wholly bad. Sin is not merely a foreign body in an otherwise pure substance; it is an infection which poisons and corrupts the entire being. Because of this fact we are condemned to eternal loss; apart from grace nothing can be done for us. Just as there may be sound spots in decaying fruit, so there may be areas of good in a wicked man; but the wickedness flavors the "good" so that it is useless for practical purposes.

The only hope for a situation of this kind is the introduction of a new life to offset the old. Salvation—or sanctification, which is salvation subjectively applied—is really the activity of resurrection life in a dead man. All that can be done with sin is to let it die. A new life must take its place.

Suppose a man is guilty of some crime and is sentenced to death. The sentence is carried out, and the man is pronounced dead by the doctors. Then suppose a new life is infused in him, and he stands upon his feet again, ready to take his part in the world. Legally, since he is dead, the old condemnation is removed and the new life gives him a fresh start. He is no longer under the former condemnation. He is ready to begin a new life, free from the hindrance of the previous record.

Precisely this thing occurs in the spiritual life of the man who believes in Christ. The resurrection life of Christ becomes the starting point of a new career for him. Bunyan in his famous allegory of the Christian life tells how Christian, the pilgrim from the City of Destruction to the City of God, was plodding along wearily, weighed down with a pack of sins on his back that hindered his progress. Finally he came to a cross, and as he looked at it, the pack fell from his back, rolled down the hill into an empty grave, and he saw it no more. The empty grave meant that the sins had been swallowed up, and that he was free from condemnation.

2. FREEDOM FROM THE COMPULSION OF SIN

The principle of the resurrection goes further still.

Not only is sin the reason for our condemnation, but it also drives us to evil. Paul says again of his inward state, "That which I do I know not: for not what I would, that do I practise; but what I hate, that I do. . . . So now it is no more I that do it, but sin which dwelleth in me" (Rom. 7:15, 17). He sees clearly that his course of life is evil. He seeks to avoid that evil and to move toward righteousness, but finds his moral strength unequal to the emergency. He sins, whether or no. This is the experience of all men who seek to resist temptation by their own strength. Yet here is a strange irony that the more a man seeks to escape from the loathsome slavery of sin, the less success he has, and the more intolerable his position becomes. Small wonder is it that this man cries out, "Wretched man that I am!" (Rom. 7:24).

Is there a remedy?

There is: the "law of the Spirit of life," which is the power of the risen Christ. The law of sin is not annihilated by that power, but is offset by it, so that man can, by the power of the Spirit of God, do the will of God.

Perhaps a parable will illustrate the point. On the land of a certain estate were a great number of trees. The land was rich and well fertilized, but under the trees no grass would grow.

The owner tried all kinds of devices to make a lawn, but to no avail; it simply would not develop. The reason for the failure was not that the grass seed was impotent nor that the soil was incapable of growing grass, but rather that the trees so over-shadowed it and so took the plant food from the soil that there was nothing left to nourish the grass.

So with us, the dominating power of the resurrection life offsets and overcomes the law of sin. The latter is still present with us. "If we say that we have no sin, we deceive ourselves, and the truth is not in us" (I John 1:8). The sin is there; but since the divine life is more powerful, it is held in check. "Wherefore, my brethren, ye also were made dead to the law through the body of Christ; that ye should be joined to another, even to him who was raised from the dead, that we might bring forth fruit unto God . . . but now we have been discharged from the law . . . so that we serve in newness of the spirit, and not in oldness of the letter" (Rom. 7:4, 6).

In this application of the resurrection life we find our daily victory. Sin is still present with us; it may in a moment of faith-lessness rise to trip us; but the new life in Christ within con-stitutes our freedom from its compelling power.

> . . . Our old man was crucified with him, that the body of sin might be done away, that so we should no longer be in bondage to sin. . . . Even so reckon ye also yourselves to be dead unto sin, but alive unto God in Christ Jesus.
>
> (Rom. 6:6, 11)

3. FREEDOM FROM CORRUPTION OF SIN

Sin is more than a defect; it is corruption. It is not like a stain or cut which mars a tapestry, but rather it is like mildew which permeates the fabric with its fungoid growth, utterly spoiling it. Nor are sin's ravages confined to the personality and experience of man; the entire creation is affected. The Scripture speaks of angels "that kept not their own principality" (Jude 6). Whatever be the offense at which this passage darkly hints, it is plain that the angelic order has been tinged by sin. Mankind racially as well as individually is steeped in sin. "Behold, I was brought forth in iniquity; and in sin did my mother conceive me," said David (Ps. 51:5). Even the physical creation has been affected. "Cursed is the ground for thy sake; in toil shalt thou eat of it all the days of thy life; thorns also and thistles shall it bring forth to thee . . ." (Gen. 3:17, 18) are the words pronounced upon the earth at the beginning of human sin.

To what extent the word "creation" should be interpreted is not clear. It must mean more than the realm of humanity; whether it includes all of the material universe is a question. One thing is certain: if the universe in which we live is a unit, no part of it can be corrupted without affecting every other part. More and more as we realize how the vast universe in which we live is composed of interacting forces, playing with and against each other, it is easier to understand how sin could affect all of it, though we may not understand fully how it does. There are hints in the Scripture that the corruption of sin is more widespread than we have even imagined.

For this corruption the resurrection power is the remedy. Note the following passage.

> For the creation was subjected to vanity, not of its own will, but by reason of him who subjected it in hope; because the creation itself also shall be delivered from the bondage of cor-

ruption into the liberty of the glory of the children of God. For we know that the whole creation groaneth and travaileth in pain together until now. And not only so, but ourselves also, who have the first-fruits of the Spirit, even we ourselves groan within ourselves, waiting for our adoption, to wit, the redemption of our body.

(Rom. 8:20–23, marginal reading)

The redemption of the body, which is the resurrection, is here equivalent to the deliverance from the bondage of corruption into the liberty of the glory of the children of God. Does this mean that the resurrection day will strike a new note of freedom in all nature? Is it not conceivable that decay and corruption everywhere may cease? Is it possible that a new world such as we have not been able to envision in our moments of wildest imagination will then effectually be born?

Perhaps this prospect borders on unfounded speculation, for that which seems reasonably probable may never become finally actual; but a world in which man becomes immortal and incorruptible and in which the processes of decay and corruption persist among other forms of life and even in the material creation seems rather incongruous. If this be carrying fancy too far, we can at least say that the corruption of sin in the world of human relations will be removed, and that the debasing and enslaving chain of cause and effect which it began will be forever done away. The resurrection will introduce a new level of life which will be distinctly superior to the old.

How can we illustrate that which "eye hath not seen, nor ear heard" (I Cor. 2:9, A.V.)?

Suppose you were a being living in a world of only two dimensions. You could move forward and backward, and from side to side, but not up and down. You would move in the space known to you like men on a chessboard, and all your consciousness would be conditioned by the rules of physical movement pertaining to two-dimensional space. Then suppose a being from a three-dimensional world stepped into yours. His very existence would be a puzzle to you, to say nothing of his activity. As he strode through your field of vision you would see only footprints appearing and disappearing in succession. His deeds would seem miraculous because he could do things in three-dimensional space that you could not do in two-dimensional space.

Perhaps the manifestation of the resurrection life will be the introduction into our present thinking of a new plane or dimension of living. This does not say that sin is only a limitation of our life rather than an offense against God; but it does mean that the introduction of divine power in its full and final effect will produce marvels in human life comparable to the marvels that we would effect in a two-dimensional world. There will be a freedom from the present limitations and an arresting of corruption that will make the best of this life pale in contrast with the glory that shall be revealed.

This freedom is not merely a dream of desire; it is a promise of certainty. God has planned the end from the beginning. "Whom he foreknew, he also foreordained to be conformed to the image of his Son, that he might be the firstborn among many brethren: and whom he foreordained, them he also called: and whom he called, them he also justified: and whom he justified, them he also glorified" (Rom. 8:29, 30).

In the eyes of God the work is already done, though we have not seen all of it finished in our experience. To the fact of the freedom from condemnation of sin we can bear ample testimony; we have assurance of that now. To the freedom from the compulsion of sin we are being introduced daily, as we find its hold on us lessening and our liberty with God growing. To that ultimate glory of freedom from its corruption we look forward, knowing that some day we shall be members of that eternal city of liberty into which there shall in no wise enter "anything unclean, or he that maketh an abomination and a lie: but only they that are written in the Lamb's book of life" (Rev. 21:27).

CHAPTER V

The Christian Dynamic

> That ye may know . . . what [is] the exceeding greatness of his power to us-ward who believe, according to that working of the strength of his might which he wrought in Christ, when he raised him from the dead, and made him to sit at his right hand in the heavenly places . . .
>
> Ephesians 1:18–20

FOR most of us the resurrection is far removed from present reality. Either it is the single event of the far distant past which has now by reason of time become almost a legend, beautiful but unreal; or else it is an article of the creed which looks forward beyond the horizon of our present life to a future of which we can scarcely conceive. Yet the historical resurrection of Christ from the dead is merely the most spectacular demonstration possible to human knowledge of the power that God is continually exercising among us. It differs from our present experience in form, not in quality. Objectively, we believe in it as an historical verity exemplified in the person of Christ and to be manifested also in that coming day when the dead in Christ shall rise. Subjectively, its power is available for us here and now under the ordinary conditions of living.

1. A NEW SPIRITUAL POWER

We make no denial of the actual historic fact when we say that this power has primary value for us in the spiritual realm. In Paul's prayer in Ephesians 1:19, 20, we read of

> . . . the exceeding greatness of his power to us-ward who
> believe, according to that working of the strength of his might
> which he wrought in Christ, when he raised him from the
> dead, and made him to sit at his right hand in the heavenly
> places.

This prayer is not for application in the future, but in the present. According to this passage, the resurrection of Christ was
no isolated event, wholly unrelated to our current affairs, like
some curio in a museum which we regard with awe and consider totally useless to our practical life. It was rather the concrete demonstration in the physical realm of the life of God
which now is applied to us principally in the spiritual realm.
Regeneration is the resurrection of the spiritual man; God's
work begins there.

Many figures for regeneration are used in the New Testament. John uses the biological figure of birth. In the third chapter of his Gospel, Jesus is quoted as saying to Nicodemus, "Ye
must be born anew" (John 3:7). As the infant enters physical
life with its potentialities unconditioned and ready for those
influences which shall shape it, so we enter the spiritual life
ready for new contacts in a new world. Peter echoes this idea,
but connects it with the resurrection when he says:

> Blessed be the God and Father of our Lord Jesus Christ,
> who according to his great mercy begat us again unto a living
> hope by the resurrection of Jesus Christ from the dead.
>   (I Peter 1:3)

The new birth is vitally linked to the resurrection.

Paul uses many figures. He urges Christians to "put off the
old man with his doings" and to "put on the new man, that is
being renewed unto knowledge after the image of him that

created him" (Col. 3:9, 10), as if the old life were an outworn garment to be replaced by a new one. He says that the Thessalonians "turned unto God from idols, to serve a living and true God, and to wait for his Son from heaven" (I Thess. 1:9, 10). He speaks of reconciliation of alienated persons, of adoption of sons, of being legally justified. Each of these figures represents some phase of salvation, but the one which he uses the most is that of resurrection. Unregenerate man is likened to a corpse, uncommunicative, unresponsive, and incapable of acting on his own behalf.

> And you did he make alive, when ye were dead through your trespasses and sins, wherein ye once walked according to the course of this world, according to the prince of the powers of the air, of the spirit that now worketh in the sons of disobedience; among whom we also all once lived in the lusts of our flesh, doing the desires of the flesh and of the mind, and were by nature children of wrath, even as the rest:—but God . . . made us alive together with Christ, . . . and raised us up with him, and made us to sit with him in the heavenly places, in Christ Jesus.
>
> (Eph. 2:1–6)

The story is told of an old Roman who once tried to make a corpse stand on its feet. After many futile attempts, he finally gave up in disgust, saying, *"Deest aliquid intus"*—"There is something lacking inside." What a corpse needs is not props, but a new life. What the unregenerate man needs is not a new philosophy of life, but an inner dynamic.

This needed dynamic has been provided in Christ. Just as the life of God offset the forces of death and restored Him from the grave, so it can offset the forces of sin that are operative in all of us. Death has not disappeared from the earth since Jesus' resurrection, but now we know that it is and always will be a beaten and doomed foe. Because He won the victory over it, it is not invincible, and it is ultimately to be completely conquered. Sin is still present with us. It has not been removed from us, but the resurrection life can neutralize its power and can make us new. Salvation is not merely an improvement of a corpse; it is a resurrection.

Furthermore, this regeneration is not merely resuscitation of a life previously extinguished, but the creation of an entirely new life. "If any man is in Christ, he is a new creature" (II Cor. 5:17). New motives, new habits, new outlook, new desires—all are created in him, and he begins to take on new activity and to move toward a new goal. Paul frequently speaks of the "new man," by which he means that the resurrection power, operating within, makes the personality into a new entity.

In some persons this power produces immediate and startling effects. Slovenly ignorance gives way to a quest for wisdom. Surly selfishness is transformed into sacrificial love. Moral depravity is turned into purity. Dishonesty is made into probity. The being of the man is so different that all see the difference in him. In other cases the effects are less spectacular, but none the less real. Outward conduct may not change so radically because they have always maintained a standard of decency, but the life is the same, nevertheless. Whether the man is saved from what he was or from what he might have been, the power is no less wonderful and no less genuine. The resurrection force is apparent in its fruitage of spirituality.

Once this new man is created by regeneration, he finds that he needs a new sphere of life. As the chick within the shell breaks through into the light and air of the outside world at

the moment of its hatching, so the Christian emerges into newness of life when the resurrection power of Christ transforms
his soul. The sixth chapter of Romans makes this clear when it
says that we who have died to sin cannot live any longer
therein, because

> We were buried therefore with him through baptism into
> death: that like as Christ was raised from the dead through
> the glory of the Father, so we also might walk in newness of
> life.
>
> (Rom. 6:4)

The resurrected man needs the resurrection atmosphere. As the
eagle cannot be content with the fowls of the barnyard, but
soars away to the peaks of the mountains and to the rarefied
heights of sunlit air, so we, once raised from the death of sin,
cannot be content with sinful associations and environs. We
rise toward God.

2. A NEW INTELLECTUAL STIMULUS

If we are to move in a new sphere, there must be a corre-
sponding effect on our thinking. The third chapter of Colos-
sians states this clearly:

> If then ye were raised together with Christ, seek the things
> that are above, where Christ is, seated on the right hand of
> God. Set your mind on the things that are above, not on the
> things that are upon the earth. For ye died, and your life is hid
> with Christ in God.
>
> (Col. 3:1–3)

The word translated "set your mind on" connotes the content
of thought rather than the process of thought. It contains the
notion that we have in our current idiom when we say, "What
is your mind on this subject?" By this question we mean,

"What is your opinion? What is the substance of your thought?" By the resurrection power, mind is directed to a new sphere and is given a new content.

For this reason, the Christian's mind no longer dwells on much of the matter that engages the mind of the unsaved man. Frivolous and unsavory literature, art that panders to the flesh, music that excites the lower passions—in short, anything that is incongruous with the standards of the Risen Christ will have no place in his thinking.

Nor does this mean an ethereal impracticality. Every worthy idea, every intellectual and aesthetic contribution to the advancement of thought can be considered and evaluated in a new light—the light of the resurrection. Our greatest music, the best art of the last nineteen centuries, our most potent political philosophies of freedom, our finest literature, all the achievements that have made life enjoyable and that have contributed to its aesthetic and spiritual uplift have come directly or indirectly from the followers of a Risen Christ.

Furthermore, the mind is by the resurrection given a new power. Several years ago the author knew a man whose education was limited, and who, until the time of his conversion, was perfectly satisfied with his limited attainments. He had apparently little interest in scholarship; and his lack of concern was revealed plainly by the manner in which he murdered the King's English. With his conversion came an awakening, and in a few years he became a preacher of power and a promising theologian. Had death not cut his career short, he probably would have become outstanding among his contemporaries. The resurrection power of God can take the man of mediocre ability and make him great in breadth and acumen of mind.

3. A NEW PHYSICAL VIGOR

Resurrection power may also be applicable to this present body.

> But if the Spirit of him that raised up Jesus from the dead dwelleth in you, he that raised up Christ Jesus from the dead shall give life also to your mortal bodies through his Spirit that dwelleth in you.
>
> (Rom. 8:11)

Many good commentators hold that this passage applies only to the ultimate resurrection, in which the "mortal body" shall be raised from death. Doubtless it may be so interpreted. On the other hand, it is a bit difficult to see why the word "mortal" (Greek *thnēta*), which means "liable to death," should be used of a body already dead. If the Spirit of God is indwelling it, how can it be reckoned as a corpse? Why limit His activity to the future resurrection as far as our physical body is concerned? We grant that both the term "mortal" and the term "make alive" used here are used also in I Corinthians 15 with definite reference to the final resurrection; but the context of this passage makes it apply to the present rather than to the future. To make the phrase "shall give life" descriptive of the Spirit's continuous work in the physical life of the believer rather than solely of the ultimate physical renewal seems preferable.

The word of God does not, of course, guarantee physical immortality to this present body. Unless the Lord comes within our lifetime, we, like all others, shall descend into the dust of death, and our bodies will be absorbed into the earth from which they came. But this text does clearly imply that the indwelling Spirit of God can and will impart new physical strength to our present body by applying to us the resurrection power of Christ. He can and will keep it in good running order until our work for God here is done.

Paul, in the Second Epistle to the Corinthian Church, alludes to some experience which happened to him in Asia, and says that he was "weighed down exceedingly . . . insomuch that we despaired even of life" (II Cor. 1:8). What the experience was, we do not know; it may have been sickness, or intense persecution, or something else. The important thing is that he put his trust not in himself, "but in God who raiseth the dead," and he was delivered for many more years of useful toil. All his life was lived by this power, for he believed God who said, "My grace is sufficient for thee: for my power is made perfect in weakness" (II Cor. 12:9).

Naturally this power is not given to us to allow us to break God's physiological laws with impunity, nor to afford license for unlimited physical indulgence. But when we have spent all in His service and at His behest, and feel that we can go no farther because of weakness, His power can renew our bodies for further usefulness even beyond what might naturally be expected of them. The Christian life renews body as well as soul.

In a measure, then, we participate in the resurrection daily. Its power is not confined to an historical fact, the resurrection of Christ, nor to an article in our creed, "I believe in the resurrection of the body and the life everlasting." This power is for our present appropriation; spiritually, mentally, and physically. Every day can be Easter for us, because "the Gospel . . . is the power of God unto salvation to every one that believeth" (Rom. 1:16).

CHAPTER VI

A Guaranteed Future

But now hath Christ been raised from the dead, the first-fruits of them that are asleep.

I Corinthians 15:20

IN THIS text are united a great fact and a great promise. Often we marvel at a beautiful symphony, and feel that we never could approximate it. We go home, and vow that we never will touch the piano again. We read some magnificent passage of literature, and become painfully conscious of the defects in the last letter we wrote. The triumphs of others only make our defeats more patent and deepen our spiritual discouragement.

If the resurrection of Christ were merely an exhibition of the divine power which can overthrow death, it might only mock us by its contrast with our own failure. Its glory consists in its being the example and pledge of what God will do for all those who have believed in Christ.

If we plant a garden in the spring, we tend it carefully and watch the little plants push up through the earth. As the summer lengthens, they mature and finally begin to bear fruit. One day we step into the garden and pick an ear of corn or a handful of beans, which we bring back triumphantly to the house as the firstfruits of our labor. Yet if that were all we were to harvest, we would be disappointed. We expect that the firstfruits will be only the promise of a larger crop to come. So

Christ is called "the firstfruits of them that are asleep." He is the sample of what awaits all of the sons whom He is bringing to glory. The resurrection, then, is a portrayal of our future.

1. VINDICATION

The resurrection is God's answer to injustice. Jesus Himself is the example. Persecuted undeservingly because of the prejudice of His enemies who were envious of Him, tried illegally, condemned to the death of a criminal slave, He was the victim of brutal injustice. In spite of the sick whom He had healed, the hungry whom He had fed, the ignorant whom He had enlightened, the seekers whom He had taught, the world—political, social, and religious—cast Him out. His earthly career ended in stark and brutal tragedy; He did not have a chance. Man passed sentence on Him without regard to principles of equity and justice, and sent Him to die on the cross of shame. Had the story ended there, we might rightfully conclude that there is no justice in the universe, since the holiest and most gracious character that has ever lived died the worst of deaths, despised and rejected by His contemporaries. But it did not end there. God reversed the verdict. In the great sermon on the Day of Pentecost, Peter made this point quite clear:

> Him, being delivered up by the determinate counsel and foreknowledge of God, YE by the hand of lawless men did crucify and slay: whom GOD raised up.
>
> (Acts 2:23, 24. Capitals ours)

The resurrection is God's final declaration of the vindication of Jesus, and the tangible evidence that justice shall prevail in the universe.

Sometimes it is hard to believe that. Greed, corruption,

violence, and hatred seem to prevail everywhere. As Shake-speare's Hamlet said:

> In the corrupted currents of this world
> Offence's gilded hand doth shove by justice;
> And oft 'tis said the wicked prize itself
> Buys out the law.[1]

The meek are obviously not inheriting the earth. It appears that right is forever on the scaffold and wrong forever on the throne. In spite of our idealism, and in spite of our desires for a new world in which justice shall prevail, we seem no nearer to it than we were a millennium ago. In particular is that true of God's people, for they are still persecuted and hated as was their Master. It is hard to understand why the righteous should suffer and why the wicked should prosper. Nevertheless, they do; and as far as human vision goes, there seems to be no answer to the riddle.

Yet there is an answer. The resurrection of Christ has shown to us that death does not end the accounting. Jesus taught that

> All that are in the tombs shall hear his voice, and shall come forth; they that have done good, unto the resurrection of life; and they that have done evil, unto the resurrection of judgment.

> (John 5:28, 29)

There is an old proverb which says: "God does not settle His accounts every Saturday night." Perhaps not; but He always settles them! The Word of God teaches unmistakably that the day will come in which every injustice, every wrong, every cruel and shameful deed shall be brought to book before the last tribunal; and correspondingly, every unnoticed kindness, every

[1] *Hamlet*: Act III, Sc. iii, lines 57–60

unappreciated virtue, every unrecognized sacrifice shall receive its reward. The seer on Patmos records for us what that day will bring:

> And I saw a great white throne, and him that sat upon it, from whose face the earth and the heaven fled away; and there was found no place for them. And I saw the dead, the great and the small, standing before the throne; and books were opened: and another book was opened, which is the book of life: and the dead were judged out of the things which were written in the books, according to their works.
>
> (Rev. 20:11, 12)

Before that tribunal humanity shall appear in person. In the searching gaze of the Eternal Majesty every secret thought and deed shall stand revealed as clearly as though illuminated by a searchlight. No excuses, no alibis, no influence, no bribes will avail at the last assize. God's saints shall be vindicated and His enemies confounded in the day of resurrection.

2. VITALITY

Suppose some genius constructed an intricate machine for the performance of some important process, and spent several years in perfecting it. Just at the point when it had been developed successfully for use, and was about to be put to doing its best work, he deliberately destroyed it. We should regard such an occurrence as an irrational tragedy, an insane caprice.

Such a tragedy is death. Over the course of the centuries God has been developing man; and through regeneration He has brought him to the point of greatest usefulness. Spiritually, mentally, and physically, the divine power has made of him the last and best of God's creation. If, then, death intervenes to cut short God's work, can it be less than a tragedy?

Scientists tell us that death is physiologically, psychologically, and philosophically unnecessary. Physiologically, there is no good reason for man to die, for his body possesses the powers of self-renewal. Psychologically, there is no reason, for as he matures his mind grows stronger and better balanced: and with the increase of maturity comes the increase of capacity and judgment. Philosophically, death is unnecessary, for man should gain in strength and not lose, if the universe is progressive and rational. Yet, reasonable or unreasonable, death is here. Its icy hand claims all of us. None, apart from the intervention of God, is exempt. God has an answer. In the resurrection the divine vitality meets human mortality, and overcomes it.

If we plant a seed in the ground, and, after an interval, dig it up again, we find that it has died. The original seed has decayed, and the moldering pulp witnesses to the fact of its death. Yet from it there will also be springing a new life which will, in time, reproduce the original form in another entity.

Similarly, the body dies. We cannot trace the continuity of life as we can with the seed; but the Word tells us that "so also is the resurrection of the dead." The green shoot coming forth from the ground may bear no external resemblance to the seed that we planted. So the new body may bear no resemblance to the one that we now have, but it will be the continuation of that inward life that we now possess, the final flowering of the resurrection life in material form.

What will the new body be like? No specific description is given, but certain general statements are given to us, and with these we shall have to be content.

It will be an *incorruptible* body. Everything on earth decays.

The adamantine rocks that seemingly defy time will ultimately split under the action of sun and water, wind and frost, and crumble away. The trees that have survived the centuries will at last wither and fall. Steel rusts to red granules, and disappears. Man himself, who can blast the rocks, or cut the trees, or erect the steel, is least durable of all. The seeds of death are in us at birth. Our body begins to die as soon as it is born, and though the forces of life for a few years hold the ascendancy over the forces of death, corruption gradually sets in, until finally the shaking hand, the trembling knee, and the dimming eye are laid in the grave.

The new body shall be raised in incorruption. Weariness, sickness, and age will be unknown to it. Constant renewal of the vital forces, whatever they are and however they may be manifested, will maintain a constant level of physical vigor and freshness. The word "physical" is used here not to indicate that the body must be exactly like this present one, made of the chemicals of earth and subject to their laws; but rather that it will not be intangible or ghostly. Jesus' body was tangible. It could be seen, felt, and heard, but it transcended the corruption of earth. He dies no more; "death hath no more dominion over him." We shall be like Him.

It will be a *glorious* body. Death is an inglorious defeat. One fragment of metal, a tiny germ, an insignificant bit of chemical can lay waste the brain and muscle that have been the instruments of great achievements. The artistry of a Phidias, the statesmanship of a Lincoln, the mathematical genius of an Archimedes, the religious powers of a Paul have no defense against this insolent destroyer. Whatever our achievements, we all subside ingloriously into the grave. Paul calls our present body a "body of humiliation," and so it is. The new body will be patterned after the body of His glory. Perhaps it will shine with the incandescence of that life which shone in Christ when He appeared transfigured to His disciples on the holy mount.

It will be a *powerful* body. Strangely enough, man has never had a body commensurate with his intelligence or its powers. The ant can in proportion to its size carry a far heavier load than a man. The grasshopper can spring farther. The bird can see better. The dog can detect sounds that man's ear never hears. Left to his own unaided powers, man is more helpless than any animal. He must be nursed longer, and cannot forage for himself until he is several years old. He has not the protection of fur against weather. He cannot make his way in earth, air or water as well as the animal, the bird, or the fish. He has not the fleetness of the deer nor the muscle of the bear. True, he has intelligence that they do not possess; but that alone against the raw elements of nature will not suffice. When at last he crumples under the strain of life he collapses as weakly as any other being. Of his body it can be said truly "It is sown in weakness," and cannot of itself command the elements.

"It is raised in power." The resurrection of Jesus showed that a new power was manifested in Him. He entered the room, "the doors being shut" (John 20:26). How? We can only speculate. Physicists tell us that matter is composed of tiny particles of force rotating about each other at an inconceivably high rate of speed, and, in proportion to their size, widely distant from each other. These are arranged as patterns to form the matter that we know.

Suppose a body could be formed by a pattern of force that did not coincide with these other patterns. The picture may be crudely illustrated by laying a dozen potatoes on a table so that all touch each other. Peas could be placed between the potatoes so that they form a definite pattern. If the potatoes could be held together as a pattern, and the peas likewise, the pattern of peas could be passed through the pattern of potatoes without disturbing the design of either. Now reduce the size of these to the minutely small, so that the spaces between them become invisible. Each pattern would appear to be a solid object, but one pattern could still interpenetrate the other without causing any visible displacement.

Will the resurrection body consist of a pattern of forces, composing a type of matter with which we are not familiar? The X-ray does something of the sort when it can pass through a solid without breaking it. There is no room for dogmatism here. The Scriptures are not specific, and we know too little about the ultimate constitution of matter to make a final affirmation of what can or cannot be. Suffice to say that the Word has promised us that this "body of our humiliation" shall be "conformed to the body of his glory, according to the working whereby he is able even to subject all things unto himself" (Phil. 3:21).

It will be a *spiritual* body. By "spiritual" we do not mean ethereal, intangible, ghostly, but rather that it will be a medium capable of expressing our finer aspirations and spiritual qualities. Our present bodies cannot convey by expression all of the things that we think and feel in the spiritual realm. There are experiences in the Christian life that cannot be reduced to words or gestures. What vocabulary will suffice to express the raptures of the soul redeemed from the bondage of sin? What songs are sweet enough to sing the praises of our Christ? By what facial expression can we perfectly mirror the love of God? True, the present body can reveal the power of regeneration, but it is at best an imperfect tool. It is "of the earth, earthy." "As we have borne the image of the earthy, we shall also bear the image of the heavenly" (I Cor. 15:47, 49). We have a right to believe that we shall be given an instrument adequate to the realization of the new joys and desires, privileges and responsibilities which eternal life brings. Fatigue, pain, disease, death, weakness, and failure will be forgotten; we shall possess the quenchless vitality of the resurrection life.

3. VICTORY

The resurrection will be victory over every hindrance that has held us back from that progress of which we have dreamed and which we have sought. There are, of course, deeper hindrances than those which are physical; and these shall be done away also. The resurrection will bring victory over incompleteness. This life leaves work only half-finished. We no sooner learn how to live than we quit living. Our dreams are unfulfilled; our work undone. There are books to be written that we have wanted to write, but shall leave unwritten. There are messages to deliver that we shall leave unspoken. There are faults to correct that will never be amended. We accomplish only a fraction of what we undertake; and that fraction is not done any too well. If the certainty of death ends all, we are doomed to abiding pessimism.

The resurrection means that we shall have an endless life in which to accomplish those tasks that have been committed to us. We shall never have to leave any work unfinished. The resurrection life will not be eternal idleness, but rather the opportunity to do new works without the interruptions, imperfections, and incompleteness which an existence subject to death entails.

The resurrection will be victory over futility. So many of our deeds, even when completed, bring no certain and abiding results. Consider Jesus' career from the human plane, apart from the resurrection. From that viewpoint, it was a failure. He died discredited in the eyes of the world, crucified as an impostor with the sarcastic inscription above His head, "This is the King of the Jews." His followers were scattered, and His teachings probably would have been forgotten in a generation except as some fragment of legend happened to be embodied in the current of tradition or in some manuscript of secondary fame. Yet from this apparent failure God wrought the most tremendous victory of the ages by raising Him from the dead. The resurrection gave a new value to all of His deeds, and even His death became a triumph in its light.

So, too, it is with us. If death ends all, then our accomplishments are a mockery, for they leave nothing permanent. At best, the deeds of one passing generation abide only to bless one or two subsequent generations, and to be repudiated, perhaps, by those farther on. The resurrection gives us an expectation of something more than futility. At the close of the long argument for the reality of the resurrection recorded in I Corinthians 15, we find this conclusion:

> Wherefore, my beloved brethren, be ye stedfast, unmovable, always abounding in the work of the Lord, forasmuch as ye know that your labor is not vain in the Lord.

True it is that

"With aching hands and bleeding feet
We dig and heap, lay stone on stone;
We bear the burden and the heat
Of the long day, and wish 'twere done:
Not till the hours of light return
All we have built do we discern." [1]

In the white light of the resurrection morning we shall see the final result of our accomplishments, and shall realize that our labors have not been in vain.

The resurrection will bring ultimate victory over sin. As long as we are in the body, we are liable to sin. The body is not sinful, but its appetites form the avenues along which temptation marches to attack the citadel of Mansoul, to borrow Bunyan's figure. There is, of course, victory over sin here and now, but the liability to sin is ever present with us. God has promised that "whom he justified, them he also glorified" (Rom. 8:30). So certain is this victory that it is regarded as already accomplished; the past tense of the verb so indicates. In the glorified body there will be no appetites that can serve as the tools of sin. The bitter struggles and agonizing humiliations of sin will be past, and we shall be forever free in righteousness. "The sting of death is sin; and the power of sin is the law: but thanks be to God, who giveth us the victory through our Lord Jesus Christ" (I Cor. 15:56, 57).

Salvation is not now complete. "Beloved, now are we children of God, and it is not yet made manifest what we shall be" (I John 3:2). We are still in a state of expectant imperfection, waiting for the day when God shall finish His work and bring in the consummation of His great purpose in Christ. When He

[1] Matthew Arnold: *Morality*

returns, hope shall become realization, and faith shall be lost in sight.

> Behold, I tell you a mystery: We all shall not sleep, but we shall all be changed, in a moment, in the twinkling of an eye, at the last trump: for the trumpet shall sound, and the dead shall be raised incorruptible, and we shall be changed. For this corruptible must put on incorruption, and this mortal must put on immortality. . . . Thanks be to God, who giveth us the victory through our Lord Jesus Christ.
>
> (I Cor. 15:51–53, 57)

The future, which alone holds the fulfillment of our hopes, is guaranteed to us by the resurrection. If we can believe that Christ arose from the dead, we can be equally certain that we who have believed in Him and who have been united to Him by that power that raised Him from the dead shall share in His final triumph when He shall come to be glorified in His saints and to be admired by all them that believe.

> "Soar we now where Christ has led,
> Following our exalted Head;
> Made like Him, like Him we rise;
> Ours the cross, the grave, the skies!
> Alleluia!"
>
> (Charles Wesley)

CHAPTER VII

An Urgent Motivation

This Jesus did God raise up, whereof we all are witnesses.
Acts 2:32

TEN unnerved and disheartened men sat brooding in an upper room in the city of Jerusalem late one Sunday afternoon. Three days before, Jesus, their beloved teacher and trusted leader, had been put to death by the joint action of the Jewish hierarchy and the Roman procurator, and they had been left to mourn His untimely fate. Fear, failure, and futility were written on their countenances. The joyous fellowship of yesterday was only a hallowed memory. The pointed parables, the sharp criticism of injustices, the penetrating imperatives of His teaching belonged to the past. The promises which He had made to them of the forgiveness of sins, of lasting peace of heart, and of a coming kingdom seemed valueless. How could One who had been "numbered with the transgressors" forgive sins? How could He give peace of heart who had died in agony upon a cross of shame? What right had He to talk of a coming kingdom when He could not save Himself? Even their faith in eternal righteousness had been shaken, for how could a righteous and sovereign God allow so perfect a life to suffer such a death as His?

Obviously their assembly could only mean the funeral of their enthusiasm. They had seemed to possess a great message and to be working for a good cause, but with the death of Jesus all had collapsed like a punctured balloon. They dared not lift their voices in His defense, for He had died disgraced in the eyes of the multitude, and it would be dangerous for them to appear as His avowed partisans. Nor could they ever be the same men that they were before they had met Him, for He had left an ineradicable impression upon their lives. The bitterness of disappointment and the bleakness of a future with only memories —and sad ones at that—robbed them of all zest for life and work.

Suddenly in the gathering gloom they became aware of a Presence. A familiar voice sounded in their ears, "Peace unto you"—and Jesus stood before them. Scarcely daring to trust their senses, they stared at Him aghast, and then at each other, wondering whether they had been seized by some strong hallucination. But no!

> "In His hands and feet are wound-prints,
> And His side."

Recognizing the scars, "the disciples therefore were glad, when they saw the Lord" (John 20:20). The reality of the Risen Christ changed their attitude completely. Sorrow was exchanged for gladness, fear for faith, and despair for hope. Past experience with Him was now a dynamic power rather than a haunting memory because He was alive.

With the appearance of the Risen Christ to the despairing men was born a new fervor which, fanned by the wind of Pentecost, brought about the establishment of the Christian church. Wherever there has been a genuine Christianity there has been a real fervor. The gospel of Christ is not a cult with which the dilettante toy idly, nor which the learned can discuss in calm detachment. Either it is true or it is not. If not, it might as well be abandoned once for all. If it is true, it demands that we shall espouse it with all our hearts and preach it with unremitting zeal to the ends of the earth. If men can become wildly excited over the election of a magistrate who, after all, is only a man and whose term of office will soon expire, should they not show some fervor over the reality of the Risen Christ, who is ordained by God to be the Savior and Judge of all men, and who is so declared by His resurrection?

1. THE MOTIVATION OF A NEW TRUTH

The message of the Risen Christ constitutes the heart of missionary preaching. Peter and John, imprisoned because they proclaimed in Jesus the resurrection from the dead, went straight back to the same preaching after their release. Paul, after an able defense of the gospel of the resurrection, concluded his argument by saying that he wished that all his hearers could be like him, "except these bonds." Only a tremendous reality could have given these men the abiding enthusiasm that drove them on through persecution and privation to the evangelization of the world. What was this reality?

The first fact in this reality is that the resurrection is the proof of the actuality of sin. Had Jesus remained in the tomb, the crucifixion might have been regarded as the judicial removal of a troublesome demagogue, or possibly as the tragic death of a beloved teacher, or, at the worst, as a gross miscarriage of justice. Whatever views be taken under the circumstances, His execution might have been regarded as the blunder of an ignorant and bigoted age. The resurrection from the dead proved conclusively that Jesus of Nazareth was the Messiah of the Jewish nation foretold by the prophets; that His claim to be the Son of God was not the idle boast of an impostor; and that the man whom Jew and Gentile had scorned and rejected was the Lord of Glory. "[Ye] killed the Prince of life; whom God raised from the dead," said Peter to the council (Acts 3:15). In that one act God revealed His everlasting condemnation of those human traits and passions which sent His Son to His death. "He showed them his hands and his feet" (Luke 24:40) as a mute but convincing evidence of what human sin had done.

The disciples were thus convinced that sin was not a theory but an actuality. Small wonder, then, that their preaching rang with appeals to repentance that fell upon the hearts and consciences of their hearers like the blows of a sledge hammer. If Christ has risen, the sin that brought Him to death must be faced and overcome. It cannot be dodged or excused; it must be met.

The resurrection of Christ is the guarantee of a real salvation. His scars speak of a finished atonement for sin. In the thirteenth chapter of Acts is Paul's well-known sermon in the synagogue of Antioch of Pisidia, probably a representative specimen of his normal missionary addresses. After a long historical argument, culminating in the narration of the death and resurrection of Christ, Paul brings his message to this climax:

> Be it known unto you therefore, brethren, that through this man is proclaimed unto you remission of sins: and by him every one that believeth is justified from all things, from which ye could not be justified by the law of Moses.
>
> (Acts 13:38, 39)

Christ risen means that the demands of the law are fully satisfied. Christ risen is the magnanimous reply of God's grace to human rebellion. Christ risen means that "He is able to save to the uttermost them that draw near unto God through him, seeing he ever liveth to make intercession for them" (Heb. 7:25).

The Risen Christ is the proof of immortality. Immortality apart from Christ is at best a dream. Men have discussed it as a possibility, reasoned that it is a probability, hoped that it might be an actuality. Yet the best and most logical presentations of it have always fallen short of reality. "Plato, thou reasonest well, but—" is the attitude of most thinkers. Jesus did not argue about immortality; He simply said, "I am the resurrection, and the life: he that believeth on me, though he die, yet shall he live; and whosoever liveth and believeth on me shall never die" (John 11:25, 26). When He rose from the grave He confirmed His own words. Immortality is a certainty in Him.

With a message like this there can be real fervor. If sin is real, men are in real danger and need to be rescued from it. If a man's house is on fire, we seek to awaken him and to save him from being burned to death. Should we be less concerned over his spiritual peril? If salvation is real, we have good news to give. We enjoy carrying good tidings to our friends; should we enjoy less the privilege of declaring eternal realities? If immortality is real, we have a note of hope for the despairing; shall we not communicate it eagerly? The reality of the resurrection message imparts a new zest to our living.

2. THE MOTIVATION OF A DIVINE AUTHORITY

It is one thing to have a message to deliver; it is quite another to have the authority to deliver it. The salesman cannot be ardent about the goods he sells, however excellent they may be, unless he is sure that he has a reliable house behind him. Doubt and fervor never go together. On what authority have we the right to traverse sea and land with the imperious declaration that man must choose the alternative of believing the message to be saved, or of rejecting it, and by rejecting be lost?

The Risen Christ is the authority for the propagation of the message. When Peter and John were asked after the healing of the lame man, "By what power, or in what name, have ye done this?" they replied:

> Be it known unto you all, and to all the people of Israel, that in the name of Jesus Christ of Nazareth . . . whom God raised from the dead . . . doth this man stand here before you whole.
>
> (Acts 4:7, 10)

The resurrection had exalted Him far above all the powers of earth to the right hand of God. Because His followers considered themselves to be His representatives, they dared to defy all lesser potentates and councils that bade them be silent.

The Risen Christ is the authority for the protection of the message as given through the messengers. Compare His utterance to them, "As the Father hath sent me, even so send I you" (John 20:21), with His reply to Pilate's boast, "Thou wouldest have no power against me, except it were given thee from above" (John 19:11). As the Father assured the Son of His personal protection until the work of the latter should be fulfilled, so Christ watched over the safety of his followers as they went about His business. For them He opened the doors of jails, directed the judgment of magistrates, and averted the axe of the executioner. Because they had the assurance that He would honor His own message, they dared to do impossibilities in His name.

3. THE MOTIVATION OF A VICTORIOUS LEADER

Men love leaders. The strong man who excels others in his mind and muscle always commands a following. As long as he is winning, men will live and die for him regardless of his cause. Whether it be Communism and Stalin, or Empire and Churchill, or any other similar combination, men today the world over are looking to the leadership of some one man to bring them to peace and prosperity and to the realization of the ideals that they cherish.

Through the resurrection we have a Leader better than all others that can be named. Neither age, nor accident, nor malice, nor failure can hold Him back. Not only have we His authority for propagating His message, but we have also His leadership in the enterprise.

See what the Scriptures say about His leadership.

He led the disciples in facing a new world. From the upper room in Jerusalem the little group went to present to a cultured and cynical age the gospel of the cross. To the Gentile, it was utter foolishness to think that so irrational a procedure as belief in a crucified Jew could assure him of his salvation. To the Jew it was blasphemy to assert that one who had been hanged on a tree could possibly be Israel's Messiah. Who of that group was able to plan a campaign that could make this strange gospel triumphant over Greek philosophy and over Jewish legalism? The Risen Christ directed them to "tarry at Jerusalem" until power should come upon them from on high. He ordered them to present their message as witnesses, not as orators. His work built the church: "The Lord working with them, and confirming the word by the signs that followed" (Mk. 16:20); "The Lord added to them day by day those that were being saved" (Acts 2:47, margin).

He led them in matters of procedure. Through His Spirit He indicated by revelation every major change of policy, organization, and itinerary. The appointment of the seven for the social service of the church, the beginning of the ministry to the Gentiles, the decision of the council at Jerusalem with regard to the status of Gentile converts, the routes to be followed in the evangelization of the Roman world were all determined by Him. He did not always preserve His servants from death, but though the workmen passed, the work persisted. He opened and shut doors for them. He emboldened them in the face of opposition. He wrung victory from defeat, until the Gospel of the Risen Lord was known, believed, and loved in every province of the Roman Empire, and from the hovel of the slave to the palace of the Caesars.

The same leadership that inspired the apostolic church to sacrificial loyalty is ours today. The Risen Christ is still marching on and beckoning us to follow. Whether in the pulpit, in the shop, in the field, or in the office, whether in the slums or in the schoolroom, whether in the sands of Arabia or in the mountains of Tibet or in the jungles of South America, whatever be our location or occupation, He calls for the same unquestioning faith and the same unwavering allegiance that He demanded from His first followers. He offers the same guidance and protection to us that He gave to them. Because He has conquered death, He leads us in the train of His triumph, and we can follow Him devotedly and jubilantly.

"Lead on, O King Eternal,
  The day of march has come;
Henceforth in fields of conquest
  Thy tents shall be our home.
Through days of preparation
  Thy grace has made us strong,
And now, O King Eternal,
  We lift our battle song.

"Lead on, O King Eternal,
  We follow, not with fears;
For gladness breaks like morning
  Where'er thy face appears;
Thy cross is lifted o'er us,
  We journey in its light:
The crown awaits the conquest;
  Lead on, O God of might."
                    (Ernest W. Shurtleff)

CHAPTER VIII

The Secret of Courage

... If by any means I may attain unto the resurrection
from the dead.

Philippians 3:11

NOWHERE in the New Testament is the power of the resurrection in the individual life better illustrated than in this thumbnail autobiography of Paul in the third chapter of Philippians. In it he unfolds to us most of his early antecedents. He was a Jew of the warrior tribe of Benjamin, and was apparently proud of his fighting blood. He was named for Israel's first king, Saul, who was also a Benjamite. He belonged to the strictly Hebraistic group of Jews who preserved the Aramaic dialect of their ancestors and the ancient Hebrew customs, even though they lived in a predominantly Greek civilization. In the interpretation of the law he held to the tradition of Pharisaism, which was ultraconservative in its ceremonial requirements. So zealous was he for the Jewish faith that he had persecuted the church even in cities outside of Jerusalem. Most amazing of all, he claimed a perfect legal righteousness, for he stated that touching the righteousness which was in the law, he was found blameless. Yet when he was arrested by Christ on the Damascus road he forgot all of these things. His passion for the law became a passion for Christ. All the advantages of birth, of breeding, of religious training, and of ecclesiastical advancement he charged off as loss. He renounced all hope of power and prestige in Judaism for the sake of the new faith that had come to him in Christ.

The letter to the Philippians was written about thirty years after Paul's conversion. Between the two points stretched a long and eventful career. He had pioneered the missionary enterprise of the Christian church from Antioch in Syria through southern Asia Minor to Macedonia and Greece. He had laid the foundation of Christian theology and of Christian literature. He had pleaded the cause of Christ before councils and before officials of the Roman Empire in the face of polite indifference and of biting sneers. He had been stoned, ridiculed, abused, and neglected. Yet he pressed on because of a divinely given fortitude in his soul that was proof against these attacks. He never wavered or faltered because he had one consuming ambition that drove him forward: ". . . if by any means I may attain unto the resurrection from the dead" (Phil. 3:11). His courage sprang from the hope that the prospect of the resurrection engendered in his soul.

The phrase as given in the Greek text is peculiar: ". . . if somehow or other I may attain to the out-resurrection from among the dead." The English preposition *of* scarcely does justice to the vigor of the language because it may mean either separation or description. We may say with equal propriety, "I will take a piece of your cake," meaning a piece *from* it, or "I will take a piece of your cake," meaning a piece of cake rather than of something else. In Paul's language, *of* means the former. He seeks earnestly a resurrection that will distinguish him from others, one that is *out from* the dead.

Certainly this does not imply that he was working for his

salvation, for in the immediately preceding context he has stated emphatically that he sought to be saved not by his own righteousness, but by that of Christ. The struggle is evidently not for salvation, of which he was already sure, but for a reward. Yet how does the resurrection constitute a reward? If all that are Christ's will ultimately be resurrected, as I Corinthians 15:22, 51-54 and I Thessalonians 4:16 imply, in what way does the resurrection constitute a reward for good works and a stimulus to fortitude? If all persons in a given class receive a certain grant, it can hardly be called a prize for excellence.

One or two hints appear in the Scriptures. In Hebrews 11:35 is a statement concerning the persecuted faithful of former days: "Women received their dead by a resurrection: and others were tortured, not accepting their deliverance; that they might obtain a better resurrection." Degrees in the resurrection are implied as a reward of suffering. The expectation of this reward is attributed not to Christians of the new dispensation, but to Hebrew believers under the old covenant; nevertheless, there would be no point in mentioning the example unless it could be followed by the readers. I Corinthians 15:23 states that each shall rise "in his own order." What constitutes the "order"? Order or rank presupposes the precedence or superiority of some. I Thessalonians 4:16 says that "the dead in Christ shall rise first," at least in time, thus taking precedence over the living. From these passages it seems fair to assume that in the resurrection there will be gradations of precedence and of reward, and that those raised out from among the others will be those whom God shall reward first for their loyalty to Him.

There is, of course, no question that the dead in Christ shall be raised long before the wicked dead. Revelation 20:4, 5 makes this clear:

> And I saw thrones, and they sat upon them, and judgment was given to them: and *I saw* the souls of those who had been beheaded for the sake of the testimony of Jesus, and for the sake of the word of God, and as many as did not worship the beast nor his image, and did not take his mark upon their forehead and upon their hand; and they lived, and reigned with Christ a thousand years. The rest of the dead lived not until the thousand years should be finished. This is the first resurrection.
>
> (Original translation)

Without digressing into the fascinating bypaths of interpretation which this text opens, we may say that it implies two resurrections. In the first resurrection will participate those who have suffered on behalf of Christ. They shall reign with Him where they previously suffered ignominious defeat; and their rising shall be called the "first resurrection." In order to establish the distinction intended here, it is not necessary to insist that this "first resurrection" is the exclusive privilege of a chosen few. It may mean simply that the resurrection of the righteous dead is separated from that of the wicked by a long interval, and that those who rise in it shall reign with Christ as associates in His kingdom. It is an "out-resurrection from among the dead" as far as the ungodly are concerned, and possibly implies some precedence of rank even among believers.

How can so remote an event as this be applied to our present needs?

The letter to the Philippians affords a practical demonstration of the fortitude created by the resurrection hope. For Paul, twenty-five or more years of exhausting labor had been brought to an abrupt terminus by imprisonment. For two years he had been held by the Roman authorities in hope of extracting a bribe from him, and he had extricated himself from an apparently hopeless position by appeal to Caesar. When he wrote the Epistle to the Philippians he had been in Rome for a somewhat longer time, possibly as much as two years, and still he had no assurance of release. His language in the first chapter sounds rather pessimistic as far as release is concerned, for he says that he is "in a strait betwixt the two, having the desire to depart and be with Christ" (Phil. 1:23). Apparently he had not yet stood trial, and was dubious of the outcome. He was in suspense, for in one breath he spoke of death and in the next spoke of "abiding" with the Philippians and of coming to them again (Phil. 1:24–26). Waiting in a situation like that with no formal charge preferred against him, and with no outward assurance as to what the future might bring, undoubtedly frayed his nerves. Yet in spite of the fact that his active life had been suddenly interrupted and that the future was clouded with uncertainty, the whole Epistle rings with a shout of joy. Anticipation of glory can carry Paul victoriously through imprisonment.

The waiting was not all he had to endure, either. The competition of rival teachers was gaining ground; and while he was hampered by confinement, they were industriously winning over his converts to their group, seeking to enhance their own reputations.

> Some indeed preach Christ even of envy and strife; and some also of good will: the one do it of love, knowing that I am set for the defence of the gospel; but the other proclaim

Christ of faction, not sincerely, thinking to raise up affliction for me in my bonds.

(Phil. 1:15–17)

It is hard to be forced to sit by idly while other men tear one's work to pieces and shatter by their insincere propaganda the results of a lifetime's labor. There are echoes of this in Paul's later Epistle to Timothy, where he says, "All that are in Asia turned away from me" (II Tim. 1:15). Evidently he never succeeded in regaining the following which was lost in some of the churches during his imprisonment. Nevertheless, he remained cheerful. He could afford to wait for the ultimate vindication of the resurrection day; and the hope of that reward enabled him to rejoice that Christ was preached, whether in sincerity or not.

A hope of resurrection sustained him in personal disappointment and conflict. There are hints in this Epistle that Paul was combating inward troubles as well as the jealous brethren who tried to gather a following at his expense and his apparently unnecessary detention by the Roman government. He spoke of "sorrow upon sorrow" that came to him with the sickness of Epaphroditus (Phil. 2:25–28), of humiliation and hunger, of destitution (4:12) and of an inward conflict produced, perhaps, by the strain of the prison years. Certainly, Paul did not possess the same physical vigor after the imprisonment that he had had before it. The enforced idleness and confinement took heavy toll of him. Yet he faced it with unfailing cheerfulness, so much so that this Epistle to the Philippians is known as the Epistle of Christian joy. He regarded all the sufferings as a privilege because through them he could enter into the fellowship of

Christ's sufferings, and so go on to the knowledge of the power of His resurrection.

In frustration and apparent failure, in doubt and in conflict, this hope of the resurrection was the source of his endurance. He held forth the word of life as the runner carried the torch and passed it on to his successor, that he might "glory in the day of Christ, that [he] did not run in vain, neither labor in vain" (Phil. 2:16). In evil times he fixed his gaze on the towering peaks of the enduring eternities. He reckoned the sufferings of the present which were incident to the fulfillment of his commission as unworthy of comparison with the glories which the resurrection morn would bring. For this he could willingly forget the things which lay behind, and press forward unto the things which lay before.

Perhaps greater fortitude is necessary to meet the apparently unnecessary frustrations of life than to meet the direct opposition of evil. The deliberate persecutions are not so hard to face because they are to be expected; Jesus promised them. The rivalry of those who should be our helpers, the unaccountable imprisonments that take us from active duty when we seem to be most needed and most fruitful, the inward sorrows and conflicts that rack our souls when we feel that we ought to be occupied with the needs of others—these are the hardest to bear. Yet the hope of the resurrection gives courage even for these, since through them we taste "the power of his resurrection, and the fellowship of his sufferings" (Phil. 3:10).

CHAPTER IX

The Ultimate Goal

> And he that sitteth on the throne said, Behold, I make all things new.
>
> Revelation 21:5

THE book of Revelation has always been a mystery to the Christian public. Much has been written concerning it that is sheer fancy; and even the sanest expositors do not agree on all points of interpretation. On one thing they do agree, that the City of God as described in the last two chapters is a picture of the final state of the Christian. "For we have not here an abiding city, but we seek after the city which is to come" (Heb. 13:14); and in this description we find "the city which hath the foundations" which Abraham sought, and "the Father's house" of which Jesus spoke.

If the City of God is the description of the ultimate destiny of the believer, two corollaries follow. First of all, if it is the goal of our expectation and the crowning blessing of our salvation, it is the great hope and animating motive of the Christian life. We are "guarded through faith unto a salvation ready to be revealed in the last time," says Peter (I Pet. 1:5). It is the true homeland where our citizenship is registered and for which we long as exiles in a foreign country. The farther we go along life's path here, the more we yearn for a sight of the eternal city. God has prepared for us this state in which His purpose of

87

redemption will have been accomplished; and we shall not be complete until we reach it.

The second corollary is this: the state of which the passage speaks is entered only by the resurrection. A careful study of the context will reveal this fact. From Chapter 19 through Chapter 21:8 we have one unbroken vision proceeding in sequence. First comes the double announcement that God hath judged the great harlot and that the marriage supper of the Lamb has come. The ungodly system of society, characterized as the harlot, is to be removed, and the society of the godly, represented as the Lamb's wife, is to be publicly acknowledged by Christ.

The conquering Christ is next revealed proceeding to the judgment of earth. The devil's emissaries upon earth are remanded to the lake of fire, while he himself is shut up in "the abyss" (Rev. 20:1, 3). Following the reign of Christ, Satan is loosed, judged, and then there is a grand final assize of the dead, the great and the small, who stand before the throne and who are judged from the books that are opened. So terrible is this judgment that "the earth and the heaven fled away; and there was found no place for them" (Rev. 20:11). Subsequent to this judgment are introduced a new heaven and a new earth, and the city of God descends among men.

That this city of God is not the abode of the blessed dead at the present time seems clear from two considerations: first, that it is introduced only after the judgment of the great white throne, and second, that it is preceded by the resurrection.

It is true that the description of the city in Revelation 21:9 to 22:5 must be regarded as a distinct section of the book. The literary structure shows that, for it begins with the phrase, "and there came one of the seven angels who had the seven bowls . . ." etc., and so is parallel in thought with Rev. 17:1. While the two sections may be parallel in structure, and in content to some extent, since the one treats of the judgment of the harlot and the other of the disclosure of the wife of the Lamb, the language of the text shows plainly that the latter follows the former in time, if time may be regarded as a factor here. The language of 21:1-6 indicates that the advent of the New Jerusalem is subsequent to the final judgment. The section 21:9 to 22:5, then, is a further elaboration of this statement. Logically it is parallel to 17:1 to 21:8; chronologically it is subsequent. If so, the New Jerusalem is not a description of the present state of the blessed dead, but rather is a picture of the final state after the completion of God's redemptive process on earth.

Again, this advent of the final state is preceded by the resurrection. In 20:4-6 there is an allusion to the "first resurrection" of those who have suffered for Christ. They are raised at the beginning of Christ's millennial reign; the rest of the dead are not raised until the close of the reign and the judgment of the great white throne. In any case, the City of God is the abode of a resurrected populace, and only through the resurrection do men enter its gates. If the resurrection means spiritual and physical regeneration, a reconstitution of the sinner into the image of God, then the resurrection is the gateway of God's final purpose for men. God will break the present world, and will remake it to His own heart's desire.

The resurrection, then, is the key to all the eternal finalities. It is a means, not an end. It is the method by which God prepares us for the full revelation of Himself that the present flesh and blood in its weakness and sinfulness cannot stand. What are these eternal finalities?

1. THE FINAL PERFECTION OF WORSHIP

All of our spiritual life is a struggle toward perfect fellowship with God. The environment of sin with its temptations and evil suggestions acts as a brake upon our Godward aspirations. Stern persistence in a heaven-bound pilgrimage is too often interrupted by dallying to pick the flowers of pleasure in forbidden fields. We may reproach ourselves afterward for having yielded to the attractive temptation; nevertheless we did yield, and we failed by that much to draw near unto God. When we do come near, we find difficulty in expressing our feelings, and the bodily needs interrupt the sequence of thought and prayer. We are worshiping through a veil behind which the form of the Divine is discernible, but because of which we do not have clear light from Him. The resurrection lifts the veil forever. "Behold, the tabernacle of God is with men, and he shall dwell with them, and they shall be his peoples, and God himself shall be with them, and be their God" (Rev. 21:3).

Throughout history God has been seeking to dwell with men. Sin has made that impossible. He descended in the garden, and found man hiding from Him in shame because he had eaten of the forbidden fruit. He descended in cloud and flame on Sinai, but the people were terrorized, and cried out: "Let not God speak with us, lest we die" (Exod. 20:19). "The Word became flesh, and dwelt among us," (John 1:14) but found no place where He could permanently lay His head. There was no room in the inn for His birth; no room in the synagogue for His preaching; no room in the temple for His teaching, for the money changers crowded Him out. He died on the cross of Barabbas and was buried in the tomb. of Joseph. The bitter irony of man's sin is that it has barred the way to the fellowship which man has needed and which God has sought. The resurrection will create a new and sinless world in which God can enter into final fellowship with man. Neither intermediary nor ritual nor symbol will be necessary for that worship. It will bring first-hand contact with God.

Beyond this, nothing further is possible in worship, except in increasing fellowship. The resurrection will make the final worship possible.

2. THE FINAL PERFECTION OF ENVIRONMENT

Unquestionably environment affects human life and conditions attitude and thought even unconsciously. A mother whose three boys left home and went to sea was bemoaning her loneliness to a visitor.

"I don't know why they left home," she said. "We tried to make it pleasant for them, and I expected them to be the comfort of my old age."

The visitor was not surprised. Over the mantel of the fireplace hung a picture of a vessel under full sail, the white foam curling under the bow and the birds of heaven wheeling above the masts. He pointed out to the mother that the silent picture had created in her sons a desire to try the life of which it spoke. They could not resist the desire which this part of their environment had aroused in them.

In many ways we are the products of our environment. If it is mean and squalid we may become coarse and shiftless. Rear children in slums, and they will take on the morality of the slums. Now and then one will rise above the surroundings like a lily out of the mud; but for the most part, human nature, like water, seeks its own level. Any parent knows that the neighborhood in which he lives has as much influence on his children as he has, and sometimes more so.

The environment of sin surrounds us here. Though we have been redeemed within, and though Christian society may form itself as an island of righteousness in a world of wickedness, the world is still too much with us. Whether it be the crash of jazz, or debasing literature, or brutalizing war, or demoralizing drink, or any of the thousand and one other evil influences around us, they tend to dull our spiritual life even if they do not definitely entrap us. Civilization is geared to sin, and even in its best productions evil motives and hypocrisies appear. We cannot escape this fact.

The City of God promises us a new environment. Whether gates of pearl and streets of gold are to be taken literally or are merely the best device that the seer could use for describing the dazzling beauties of what he saw in the vision is beside the point. In any case, God plans to give to the resurrected believers an environment that will embody the purity and beauty of the spiritual life that He has implanted in them. For the new life there will be surroundings that shall be uncorrupted and incorruptible. It is founded on the work of the apostles and prophets, and the society is restricted to those whose names are written in the Lamb's book of life. The resurrection will be the last stage of God's preparation of his children for inhabiting the new

world. It will end forever the old environment of sin; it will be
a birth into a clean and wonderful new world.

3. THE FINALITY OF PERFECT SATISFACTION

One of the chief values of life is satisfaction of desire. Satisfaction of desire is not in itself an evil; it is only an evil when
desire usurps the place of God. The legitimate appetites of life
bring pleasure when they find their answer in gratification. As-
suredly, the City of God will not, like the Mohammedan Para-
dise, bring the unlimited satiation of every lust and craving that
we have here. Jesus pointed out that in the resurrection our very
constitution would change, and that we would no more have
fleshly appetites than a butterfly would crave a caterpillar's life.
On the other hand, the tree "yielding its fruit every month" of
which Revelation 22:2 speaks probably depicts pleasures that
will be eternal and that will never cloy. Satisfaction without
satiation, enjoyment without boredom will be our lot.

Yet satisfaction does not consist merely in the gratification of
desire; it is of farther reach than that. It extends into the constructive activity of achievement. Man desires to paint the perfect picture, or to write the perfect musical composition, or to
build the perfect cathedral of which he has dreamed. Revelation
is more conservative than our dreams; but it contains all this
in the pregnant phrases, "there shall be no curse any more,"
and "his servants shall serve him."

"There shall be no curse any more" (Rev. 22:3). This is a
direct allusion to Genesis 3:17–19: "Cursed is the ground for
thy sake; in toil shalt thou eat of it all the days of thy life;
thorns also and thistles shall it bring forth to thee; and thou
shalt eat the herb of the field; in the sweat of thy face shalt

thou eat bread, till thou return unto the ground; for out of it wast thou taken: for dust thou art, and unto dust shalt thou return."

The curse is not labor, for man had that before he sinned; it is rather futility. Struggle as he may, he can do no more than hold his own. Weeds and pests, flood and sun fight against him, and he ends his life wondering whether he has done more than prolong an existence of drudgery. All this will be changed in the world which the resurrection opens. The curse is removed, which means that labor shall bring its full reward without hindrance or failure. If the farmers could be sure that every seed would yield its full crop, if the industrialist could be sure that there would be no loss by breakage or failure, if every effort produced its due result, how blessed it would be! In the coming economy of God just this is promised.

"His servants shall serve him" (Rev. 22:3). The ultimate state will not be one of balmy inactivity. It is a mistake to visualize heaven as a place where disembodied spirits float on clouds, twanging harps and singing aimlessly forever. Such a description as this is a caricature, not a picture of the truth. The text calls for constructive activity, for the service of God will call for something more than a sort of celestial cheering section. True, there will be worship and praise of God with a reverence and devotion that we never have known on earth; but there will be other activity as well. What it will be we do not know. It is idle to guess whether we shall be missionaries to other worlds, or whether we shall be engaged in the exploitation of a new kind of world with resources and powers of which we have never dreamed. That remains to be realized, and doubtless God has kept His secrets that He may delight us with His surprises when they shall be disclosed. Of one thing we may be sure: our labors will be of positive and lasting value. To this life of final achievement the resurrection is the gate.

One thing more remains: this satisfaction will never end. "They shall reign for ever and ever" (Rev. 22:5). We have a proverb that "All good things come to an end." In this life they do. The delight of today's celebration is forgotten in the toil of the morrow. The satisfaction achieved in today's conquest may be eclipsed by the humiliation of tomorrow's defeat. The institution which one man builds laboriously and triumphantly may fade or collapse under his successor. Success and failure, victory and defeat, achievement and frustration follow each other like the waves of the sea with the valleys between. There is no unbroken and unending progress in any single direction; but in the City of God we shall progress from glory to glory. Reigning implies unbroken continuity in the life of triumph.

This is God's resurrection finality; but while it is the finality of earth's story, it is only the beginning of what redemption has to offer us. The seer of the Apocalypse was not able to put into words all that he saw, and the pictures that he painted in the most vivid colors of human language that he could command do not do justice to the reality. Yet the reality is not unbelievable. If we can believe in the physical resurrection of Jesus Christ from the dead, we can believe in the resurrection of a world, for the principle involved is the same. If we have tasted the power of God in our personal regeneration and His fellowship in our lives, we can be assured that He will do on a cosmic scale what He has done for us individually. He "begat us again unto a living hope by the resurrection of Jesus Christ from the dead" (I Pet. 1:3).

As Bunyan's pilgrims took new courage when from the peaks of the Delectable Mountains they saw in the distance the shining towers of the Celestial City, so we, in a moment of spiritual vision, may take courage because in a world of wickedness and war we have caught a glimpse of the City of God, the final glory of the gospel of the resurrection.

> "Jerusalem the golden,
>   With milk and honey blest!
> Beneath thy contemplation
>   Sink heart and voice oppressed.
> I know not, O I know not,
>   What joys await me there;
> What radiancy of glory,
>   What bliss beyond compare.
>
> "O sweet and blessed country,
>   The home of God's elect!
> O sweet and blessed country
>   That eager hearts expect!
> Jesus, in mercy bring us
>   To that dear land of rest;
> Who art, with God the Father
>   And Spirit, ever blest."
>   (Bernard of Cluny)